A Life Set Free

A LIFE SET FREE — by Rena Groot

©2019 Rena Groot, Penticton, BC.

First edition 2019

Printed in Canada

ISBN 9781092493482

Cover and page layout by Brian Rodda.
www.brianrodda.ca

Contents

Acknowledgements

ThankYou, my precious Lord Jesus, for pulling me out of darkness into Your amazing light. Thank You that the law of the Spirit of life in Christ Jesus has set me free from the law of sin and death. I love you now and forever. It is You, Lord, who gave me this story and inspired me to write it. I dedicate this book to You for Your glory.

Thank you, Dr. Hendrik Jan (John) Groot, for your love, support and encouragement over the years. It is because of you that a lot of this book could be written.

Thank you, Brian Rodda, my amazing graphic designer, for making this book look beautiful. Brian says he has a black belt in graphic design. I believe him.

Thank you, Dr. Wyman, my dear Seminary professor, for proof-reading my manuscript and writing the foreword.

Thank you, Karen Davis, for editing my manuscript. Karen is an extremely busy worship leader and recording artist. I am so honored she took the time to do this. Her next musical project, "Shirei Netzach" (Songs of Eternity) will be released this year. I know it will be a blessing to multitudes.

Thank you to all the precious people who read this manuscript and wrote comments. I must say I am overwhelmed by your kind words.

Thank you to all the people who made this book possible by your roles in this story. As much as possible I have permission from people to tell you about them.

Comments

What you are about to read comes from the heart of someone I know very well. Rena is genuine, sincere and her motives are not self-seeking. They are kingdom seeking. Her words come from a place of authenticity. She loves God and seeks to honor and glorify Him.

> *Dr. H. J. Groot*
> *Penticton, BC*

A book that will bring healing, hope, and many to the very heart of Jesus.

> *Lynne Broccolo*
> *Penticton, BC*

A true story of God's love, protection and faithfulness..

> *Joyce Wiersma*
> *Summerland, BC*

How wonderfully God redeems and restores a life given to Him! I have loved following Rena on her God adventures. She is passionate in her pursuit of God and in her pursuit of souls. Her zeal and joy and courage shine through every page as does her determination to obey the Lord's promptings. This kind of a walk with God has been developed in the narrow-gate-walk that leads to life. I have been encouraged and challenged to do the same.

> *Marianne Agren*
> *Calgary, Alberta*

Rena and I have known each other for many years and shared many experiences in our journey of life. A Life Set Free is a story of God's faithfulness in her journey.

> *Evelyn Bakker*
> *Edmonton, Alberta*

A Life Set Free is an encouraging read. It is about the author's early life of rejection and loss and how she found the freedom and joy that exudes from her today as she freely spreads the gospel around the world.

> *Inez Mitchell*
> *Penticton, BC*

A touching story of seeing how one's painful past can be used to make a difference for eternity. Neglected and abandoned as a child, Rena tells how she eventually encountered Jesus and made a 180-degree turn to follow Him. To live for Jesus became her desire and telling others about her Savior became her passion. Knowing Rena personally, she models the biblical command, "You shall love the Lord your God with all your heart, with all your soul, with all your strength and with all your mind, and your neighbor as yourself" (Luke 10:27).

Anne Feenstra
Abbotsford, BC

I was captivated by the story of your life. Reading this book was like catching up with a dear friend and also like being struck by God with a 2x4. It makes me realize how much more I could be doing in the Lord's service if only I would open myself and trust Him more, as you have done. This account of your life has convicted me to allow God to work in my life as well, but not in a nagging way, more just because I want to see God's adventures the way that you have. God has taken someone society would consider damaged and used you to raise up others in ways that we may only realize in heaven. You are living as a colourful thread in God's tapestry and I can't help but feel that I am missing out on such beauty and joy. If only we would all say yes to God the way you do, what other colours would appear? Thank you for writing this book to inspire your readers. I would recommend this to others who need to hear God's voice in their lives.

Diana Smith
Hay River, NWT

A Life Set Free is a compelling story of God`s eternal love and faithfulness. Those who have been rejected, abandoned and unloved will find this to be a revealing story of how God can create great hope and purpose out of the darkness of loneliness and despondency. This book is written for "a time such as this", where hope and a future are being swallowed up with the reality of anxiety and despair. For those "seeking a way out" of the endless cycles of life's disappointment this book is for you!

Sid Waterman B. Ed; M. Div.
Missionary, Pastor, Author,
Grief Counselor
Penticton, BC

Foreword

When Rena and John Groot came to Cochrane, Alberta to study at the Canadian Southern Baptist Seminary, they brought with them a great deal of experience in working in Christian camps and mission endeavors. It was my privilege to have both John and Rena in classes in faith development and childhood education. Both were eager learners and contributors to class discussion.

Over time, I learned some of the story of neglect which Rena shares in *A Life Set Free...a true story about the love and faithfulness of God.* Reading the book, however, made me marvel again at just how much of a miracle it is that a child so neglected during her very formative years should be such a passionate sharer of the love of Christ.

Rena possesses a highly unusual sensitivity to the leading of the Lord in her life. Most readers will react, as I did, to the spontaneity with which Rena responds to opportunities to go to other countries to learn and serve. It is very natural to say "I couldn't do that." Rena's story says to us, "You might give it a try."

When I asked Rena the purpose of her writing, she answered simply, "God wants me to do it". As a reader of the book, one is encouraged to ask "What is God telling me to do?"

Barbara W. Wyman, Ph.D.
Cochrane, Alberta

A Life Set Free

"Therefore if the Son makes you free,
you shall be free indeed."
John 8:36

This story was started while sitting under a mosquito net in China. Two years later I am finally putting all the scribbly notes onto my iPad at a guest house in Haifa, Israel. It took several years for God to prepare my heart to write this story. I could not have written it sooner. It is written from a place of forgiveness, healing, wholeness and freedom.

Following God has been an incredible adventure. All glory and honor and praise to Him, now and forever. This is a true story about the love and faithfulness of God.

This is the story of a life set free.

Rena Groot

I had a desperately lonely childhood
I felt abandoned
rejected
unloved

years living
in other people's homes
convinced me
I was
the outsider
not belonging

so alone

It sounds crazy
but
I am thankful

I praise God
because
He used
everything
to give me
a greater heart of compassion
for others

Fast forward

as a 21-year-old university student
I was disillusioned with life

I felt like there was a dark
black
empty
hollow space
growing inside me
The emptiness
darkness and
hopelessness
of my life

overwhelmed me

I decided I had nothing to live for

It seemed suicide was better than living

I contemplated jumping out of a window
on the 18th floor
of an apartment building

While looking at that window
deciding what to do
I had a vision
I don't know what else to call it

It was so strange
this is hard to explain

It had been a cloudless day
but now thick clouds seemed to appear
Just outside the window
obscuring everything
I knew they weren't really there
Yet I could see them

I could see through the clouds
and I saw a throne

I could not see His face
but I knew the One
seated on that throne
was Jesus

I knew He was crying
for me
because of the pain and sadness
and brokenness of my life

He spoke
not with words I could hear

but with words
that resonated inside me

"Rena,
This is not My plan for your life.
If you turn your life over to Me
I will bring more beauty out of your life
than you could possibly imagine at this moment."

Then
Incredibly
In a split second
I saw my entire life

It was kind of like seeing a high speed video

It was too fast to see details
Yet
I had the impression that it was
an amazing
incredible
beautiful life

Obviously...
I chose to live

This next part
the unveiling of the "video"
was a process

I began searching for God

Everywhere

He seemed to be hiding
I couldn't find Him

Finally
Thankfully

there was a random invitation
to an obscure prayer meeting

and
I found Him!!!
I was broken-hearted
that I had grieved Him

I repented of my sins
and asked Jesus to be
my Lord
and Saviour

Because of His grace
and mercy
I was forgiven

I became a child of God
Adopted into His beautiful
forever family

No longer alone

Such amazing love

If I had died that day
I would have missed
Out on so much
He wanted to do in my life
and throughout eternity.

This is the story of God's amazing grace in my life.

He saw a sad
lonely girl

In His great love
and compassion

God pulled me out of darkness

into His amazing light

He has given me a hope and a future
A beautiful life

The law of the Spirit of life in Christ Jesus
set me free from the law of sin and death.

I found Him
Yet
I am seeking Him still…

This is my story.

My Grandmother

"A Word fitly spoken is like apples of gold in pictures of silver..."
Proverbs 25:11

Life seems a juxtaposition of many puzzle pieces. I used to wish I had been given different pieces, or even a different puzzle, but now I am so thankful for every moment God has given me to live. Some of the pieces are very interconnected. For example, the chapter called Circle Square Ranch happened before, during and after the arrival of our children. So even though the times sometimes overlap by the time you get to the end of this story it will all make sense. I promise you will see a picture so amazing and beautiful only God could have put it together.

Rena Groot

I was born in Vancouver, British Columbia. My mother smoked and drank while she was pregnant with me. I consider the fact that I do not have fetal alcohol syndrome a miracle. I lived with my Grandmother until I was four. I do not know why I did not live with my parents. I found out years later that my brother Roy also had lived there. I have no memory of him. Roy was one year older than me and went to live with another family when I was very young. When I was in my twenties I found out I had a brother. I phoned him and the first thing he said is, "Where have you been all my life?" Roy remembered me. I am sad for the lost years but I am glad I have him now.

My grandmother, Helen (Illonke) Hollaender Katz, had a very serious expression but when she smiled her face lit up and that is when her loving, kind eyes showed up. Thankfully I seemed to make her smile a lot. I was a skinny child which must have been an enormous embarrassment for my grandmother. She was a Jew from Eastern Europe and in her culture if you were chubby it proved you had enough wealth to buy food. Grandmother gave me an addiction to chocolate. She would cut a sandwich into tiny pieces and reward me with a piece of chocolate for each tiny piece I ate. My memories of my grandmother are the smell of her garlicky chicken soups and the pungent smell of mothballs in her closets. I remember thinking sleeping on her bed was what it probably felt like sleeping on a cloud. She had huge feather duvets to sleep on top of and to pile on top of me. It was pure amazingness.

We lived by English Bay. Grandmother owned a row house on a city block. I remember going off to explore the tide pools and bringing back treasures to share with her. Poor Grandmother. She must have been incredibly patient to have starfish and other critters deposited in her bathtub. Rather than just throw the critters away she would take them back to the ocean and free them for me to find another day. My grandmother was an artist. Where she grew up ladies were not taught to cook or clean. That was for the maids. She knew how to sew, embroider, and paint. Those were not extremely helpful talents to have when she tried to establish her own home in Canada. Grandmother reminded me of a walking art gallery. Her clothes were hand made and beautifully embroidered, right down to the matching handbags and hats. She designed and sewed my clothes. The clothes she made looked like the beautiful designer clothes I see in shops now like Laura Ashley. At the time I did not appreciate the work and beauty she put into my garments because they made me stand out from all my friends who probably wore jeans and tee shirts.

Grandmother would sit me down with colored pencils and a bowl of flowers and tell me to draw what I saw. I remember her looking at my picture and sternly admonishing me to really look at the flowers. I think she forgot I was only four. When the picture was finally acceptable I remember my grandmother's words of praise. The verse, "A word fitly spoken is like apples of gold in pictures of silver," makes sense to me when I think of my grandmother's smiling words of approval.

My grandmother loved plants. She had what seemed to me a huge jungle growing in her living room. The plants were higher than my head. I think this contributed to my love of huge plants in my home. I was in my teens when my grandmother moved to San Diego, California. Once I visited her during fig season and you would never guess what I was served several times a day. It is a miracle I still love figs. While walking around Haifa, Israel and seeing all the beautiful fig trees I could not help but wish my grandmother had moved to Israel instead of San Diego. She would have loved it.

I never really recovered from being a frail baby. When I was four it was discovered that the reason I was so skinny was because I had a growth in my throat that made swallowing difficult. It was decided that the best place for me to have the surgery to remove the growth was at the Sick Children's Hospital in Toronto. I was flown to Toronto for surgery and this is where the next chapter begins. The picture in Chapter One of this book is me at Sick Children's Hospital in Toronto waiting for surgery.

I have an amazing story to tell you. My grandmother passed away in a hospital in San Diego. I had written her a letter telling her about Heaven trying to inspire her to want to be there. I told her it is incredibly beautiful, that the gardens are amazing and she would love it. I was so sad to hear of her death as I had no assurance she believed me. A friend suggested I ask God to show me if she was in Heaven. I thought that was kind of an absurd thing to ask God but my motto is 'nothing ventured, nothing gained.' So, without much faith that there would ever be an answer I asked God to please show me where my grandmother would spend eternity. Shortly after that prayer my mother called from San Diego and told me she thought Grandmother was now in a better place. My mother was not a Christian. I told her that my grandmother was not in a better place unless she asked Jesus to forgive her sins and be her Saviour. My mother said that some men from some gospel business thing had come to the hospital and visited. She said after they left my grandmother seemed to be at peace. What a miracle. That was the answer I prayed for. I rejoice that one day you will meet my grandmother. You will love her. She may give you chocolates and garlicky chicken soup and ask if you would like your heavenly garments embroidered.

My Father

*"Nothing in all creation is hidden from God's sight.
Everything is uncovered and laid bare before the eyes of Him
to whom we must give account."*
Hebrews 4:13

Sydney Finney alias Reno Taylor

L ife is full of choices. No one in their right mind wakes up one day and says I want to see how many stupid decisions I can make today. The choices just jump out at us without warning, and without thinking we make decisions that affect the rest of our lives. The day that changed everything for my father was the day he chose to kill a man.

They called it manslaughter. They said he did not plan it and that it just happened in a fit of rage. Someone let a door slam in his face so he beat a man to death. Maybe there was more to the story? I will never know. I think I was was four years old. Because of his choice to give in to a moment of temporary insanity my father spent seven years in Kingston Penitentiary. I never saw him again.

I am ashamed to confess this about my father. It makes me feel less because others have fathers that are so much more. I am not sure if I should even be telling you this. We are supposed to respect our parents. Does telling you this horrible story about my father mean I am disrespecting him? If so, I apologize, but you needed to hear that part of the story to understand why my life took such strange turns.

After the surgery, my mother had to work to support us so I was left in the care of the very elderly, stodgy Mrs. Diamond. She ran the boarding house we lived in and I had the distinct feeling she despised children. That was in the era when children were supposed to be seen and not heard. To be fair I must have been a trial to her. My grandmother had given me an independence that would never exist today. I was free to roam to English Bay and play in tide pools and wander back to my grandmother's place with all my treasures. Grandmother said I used to collect the neighbourhood kids and sit them down on the sidewalk and have a lesson about my starfish and other tidepool treasures. So, it really was not my fault I had no idea I was supposed to ask Mrs. Diamond permission to take her cat for a walk. The fact that her cat did not want to go for a walk so I had to chase him around the coal cellar in the basement to try to capture him did not seem naughty to me. I saw people walking their pets on leashes so I thought I must put a rope around the cat's neck. I meant no harm. The cat was unscathed, but I think Mrs. Diamond was certain I was planning mayhem and murder with her coal dust covered cat. She was unimpressed. I never did get to walk her fat, fluffy, tabby cat.

The final straw for Mrs. Diamond was the day I decided to go to the corner store to buy my dad some socks. I knew he was far away and for some inexplicable reason I thought he might need socks. Of course, I did not think to tell Mrs. Diamond about my plan. Maybe I kept her in the dark on purpose as she seemed to disapprove of so much I did. My little shopping idea seemed like such a small thing but this seemingly innocent decision changed the direction of my life.

I excitedly walked to the corner store with my coins in hand. There are some things that happen in life that are burned on your mind forever. This is one of them. As I walked I noticed a man sitting on the curb. I thought he looked lonely so I sat down beside him to say hello. That is when I noticed he had no socks on. I invited him to come to the store with me so I could buy him socks. We walked to the store where the clerk kindly said my coins were just enough for socks. I might have had a few pennies. To show his gratitude my friend invited me to go to his house for milk and cookies. I still recall the euphoria I felt. My new friend had socks, and I was getting milk and cookies. Could life get any better? While walking along together my friend suddenly turned to me and with a grotesquely distorted face yelled, "RUN!!! GET AWAY FROM ME!!!" I believe God was protecting me because my friend obviously was not planning milk and cookies. I wonder if that man's conscience would not allow him to hurt me. I was in complete shock as I started running down the street. I had no idea where I was. Meanwhile, Mrs. Diamond had no idea where I was either so she called my mother to leave work and come find me. It took my mother hours of frantically searching the streets of downtown Toronto to find her lost little five-year-old. Just imagine a little girl crying and wandering the streets of Toronto. I must have had big angels walking with me that day.

Naturally, once my mother found me Mrs. Diamond wanted nothing further to do with me. I do not blame her. Mother had no option but to take me to work with her. I remember playing on a typewriter at Wolf Transmission oblivious to the chaos I brought to my mother's life. I think my mother must have been desperate for any solution. She was only 25 years old, her husband was in jail, she had no one to care of me and she was alone in a big city. Her boss suggested I stay with his daughter's family in the country until my mother could make other arrangements. That was the beginning of my living with other families for several years. I do not blame my parents. I am sure if they could they would go back and make different choices.

I am not sure how long I stayed in the first home. I remember being terrified there. It is unfortunate the boss forgot to tell my mother his daughter was psycho. The place smelled like boiled cabbage and urine. I remember being told if I was naughty I was going to be thrown down a well in the yard. I don't remember sleeping there. I think I lay awake each night with post traumatic stress disorder. I had lost my beautiful grandmother, my tidepools, my mother, my father, Mrs. Diamond's fat cat and I was with people threatening to murder me if I did not behave. Could life get any worse? No five-year-old should ever have to go through such horror or live with such people.

One happy day my mother came to collect me. I was relieved to leave the smells and the scary well that disobedient children were thrown into. But sadly, my mother had no plans to keep me. I was five when I was sent to live with the Zema family in Scarborough, Ontario. I am not sure how my mother found these people. I admit they were nice when they were sober. They had a girl a year older (Avely) and a girl a year younger (Wendy) than me. I remember the parents having drunken screaming fits and hurling plates at each other. It was a very stressful place to live. When I was naughty, and that seemed to be often, I was made to eat dry hot powdered mustard powder and sleep in the dark, dank, unfinished basement. In case you did not know, unfinished basements are a source of terror to a five year old. Those were some of the longest and scariest nights of my life.

The Zemas went to a Catholic church. That is when I first started to trust in God. I had to have naps in the afternoons and often I would just lie there and watch the curtains blowing in the breeze while flashes of sunlight danced across the walls. I would just lie there and feel God's Presence. I knew He was with me.

 I remember being so excited to start school when I was six. I loved school even though I had the distinct impression the teacher did not like me. Maybe somebody told her who I was. A nobody. A child who did not belong. The daughter of a murderer. Living with people who said she was naughty, a burden and a bother. I remember standing in the hall a lot that year. Maybe that is why I have such compassion for children. I remember the shame of being left in the classroom on the last day of school while the other children went outside to eat ice creams with the teacher as a farewell gift. Maybe I was a basket case from the trauma I had already experienced? I am sorry that teacher did not show me love and compassion, but I am thankful that because of that experience I could never shame or humiliate a child. The memory is too vivid.

It was New Years Eve, 1960, during the Cold War. Air raid sirens seemed to be blaring incessantly in Scarborough, Ontario because people were afraid the Russians were about to attack. Maybe that is what drove people to drink? The Zemas were out celebrating New Year's Eve but as they were driving home their car had a flat tire. Mrs. Zema was inebriated. She tried to flag down a trucker to help them and instead walked in front of the truck and was killed instantly. I cried with the family. I did not realize this meant I would be leaving.

The next puzzle piece was about to be put into place. Aside from being with my precious grandmother this next piece is the only beautiful piece from my childhood. The Morgans were loving, kind, godly people. They had two adult daughters, Florence and Yvonne. Mr. Morgan built a boat and named it after me. The Morgans loved me like their very own child. I desperately wanted friends so I told the children at school it was my birthday party and they were all invited. There didn't seem to be much enthusiasm so I kept embellishing the story and said there would be a clown and there would be kittens to give away. Obviously the dry hot mustard at the Zemas did not cure me from being a liar. There was no party. It was not my birthday. The Morgans and I went camping that weekend at Algonquin Park and when we returned there was a birthday gift sitting on the step. One little girl believed me. Bless her heart. Mrs. Morgan made me take the gift back to the girl's house and apologize for the lie. The little girl's mother insisted I keep the gift. It was the first time in my life I did not want a gift.

I remember the Morgans taking me to a beautiful old church with huge stained glass windows. I firmly believed in God by now. Once a little boy and I got into a verbal fight in the Sunday school class because he dared say there was no God. I was incensed that he doubted God's existence. The Morgans were from Newfoundland. Mr. Morgan had worked in the coal mines and the coal dust had settled in his lungs. I did not know he had tuberculosis and emphysema. I just knew he coughed a lot. I only lived with that beautiful family for one year. Sadly, Mr. Morgan died while I was there. Mrs. Morgan must have been grief stricken. Mr. Morgan was such a kind man.

When I was in my twenties I randomly remembered their address in Scarborough, Ontario and had the impulse to write Mrs. Morgan. She replied that she still had a note taped on her mirror that I had written her when I was seven years old. It said, "Jesus loves you and so do I". She was so happy to hear that I was a school teacher in a Christian school and I loved God. The next letter shortly after that was from her daughter Yvonne. The letter said Mrs. Morgan had passed away. Yvonne sent a ring that her mother wanted me to have. I had written her just in time to thank her for the love and kindness she showed me.

My mother then packed me off to the next family, the Springers. My first impression was this was a lovely family. I was excited to live on a farm in the country. They had a little girl who seemed pleasant, two dogs and a monkey. What could be better? I have often wondered if they ever regretted how they treated me. Again, I really wonder how my mother found these people.

The first morning I awoke at the Springers' home I was hopeful this was going to be a happy place to live. That first morning there were two chairs placed at the foot of my bed. Mrs. Springer and her daughter sat on those chairs wordlessly staring at me. It was totally weird. My happy feelings dissolved. I don't remember exactly what happened at the Springers. I realize now I lived an almost Cinderella existence, with me in a small bed in the attic and the daughter in a room that looked like it was made for a princess. Even though she could not read the daughter had a wall of books. I was not allowed to touch her books, but at night I would sneak downstairs and nab a book. (Please do not tell the Springers.) I had to read by flashlight under the covers so I would not be seen and had to finish the book that night and return it before morning so it would not be missed.

There were some highlights to living with the Springers. Geronimo was a half German shepherd and half wolf. He had gorgeous white eyes. We loved each other. We spent hours exploring and searching for rats in the old barn and frogs in the creek. Susie was a beagle who was a tick magnet. She used to leave mice and rats and other critters on the back porch for us just to show her family she loved us and wanted to provide for us. There was an abandoned orchard that seemed like an exquisitely beautiful cathedral to me. The apple and pear trees grew in such a way that the sun's rays pierced the darkness with shafts of light. It was such a peaceful place. I was the reigning princess with my Queen Anne's Lace crown and Geronimo my faithful friend.

Once, before my mother came to visit me, I was given an apple and a sandwich before her arrival. I remember thinking it was the most beautiful meal I had ever seen. I don't know what I normally ate. The Springers treated me with kindness the day before my mother's arrival. I would think everything was going to be fine now so when my mother would ask me how things were I would say everything was great. The Springers would be kind for the day, but as soon as my mother left their faces would change and I would realize nothing had really changed. I am not sure why I was so easily duped.

This is the saddest story about my stay with the Springers. Once on a visit to my mother's home in Toronto I was sitting in the bathtub when my mother walked in. She asked why I had so many bruises. I had to think quickly to fabricate a reply. The truth was Mr. Springer had asked me to rake a huge back yard full of leaves. After a while my hands were blistered and sore. I found Mr. Springer and explained that I could not finish the yard because I could no longer hold the rake. Somehow, I thought he would be compassionate. It was not his day for compassion. His response was to take me to the barn. I guess he didn't have anything else that was suitable to use to teach me not to be so rebellious so he used the crop of his whip on me. So, when my mother saw the bruises she was understandably concerned. I reasoned if I told her the truth she would take me back there (because I assumed she did not have any other options) and tell them not to hurt me anymore and as soon as she left they would kill me. I told her I fell out of an apple tree I had been climbing. She believed me. I'm not sure how I survived the Springers' home.

Shortly after that visit my mother decided she wanted to settle down and have a "real" family. She had met a man, one of my father's friends from Kingston Penitentiary, who she thought would be a suitable dad. She was only 29 when they decided to move in together. I was nine. Larry was a man desperately in need of God. I lived with them four years. During that time we moved from Toronto to Sarnia to Vancouver Island to East Vancouver. My baby sister Dawn was born in Duncan on Vancouver Island. I recall going to a second hand store and telling them I had a new baby sister and she needed clothes. They gave me bags of clothes for her for a few dollars. She was so adorable. While living in Duncan some children told me my reclusive neighbour lady was a witch. I did not believe them so I went over to say hello. The witch turned out to be a beautiful, elderly Christian lady. She took me to church with her. I remember going to the front and asking Jesus to be my Saviour. That is about the time when all Hell broke loose in my life.

I wish I could erase my twelfth and thirteenth years. I had to have emergency surgery to remove my appendix and a tumour. Larry and my mother had brought a young man escaping from an institution in Ontario with us to British Columbia. I will spare you the details of why I wish I had never met him. By the time I was thirteen it seemed like all the built up rejection and horror of my life hit me. I became incorrigible. I skipped school, hung out with druggies in East Vancouver, and basically was swiftly heading down the wrong path. I despised Larry. I thought he was a horrible man. I blamed and hated my mother for all the years of abandonment and abuse I had endured.

Once when I was thirteen Larry yelled at my mother and looked like he was going to hit her. He had been a boxer and was a huge man. My mother was barely five feet tall. I reasoned if he hits her he will kill her. So, I jumped between them and yelled at him to leave her alone. That was not one of my wisest decisions. All the rage on his face that had been directed towards my mother suddenly turned towards me. I think Larry was too shocked and surprised to react. He stood frozen to the spot while I ran to my room, climbed out the window, raced down the fire escape and ran to my grandmother's house. I stayed there for weeks. It was around that time my mother realized it was not working for Larry and me to live in the same house. Larry told my mother I was making passes at him. That was an utterly repulsive idea to me. My mother chose to believe Larry. She spoke with a social worker and started the process of having me placed in a home for juvenile delinquents as a permanent ward of the government. That brings us to the next puzzle piece.

Rescued

"Do not fear for I have redeemed you,
I have called you by name
You are Mine."
Isaiah 43:1

Have you noticed that sometimes God moves very quickly? The week my mother was to sign the papers for me to become a permanent ward of the government my mother's sister (Alice Katz Eaton) came for a work related meeting to Vancouver from Alberta. She and my mom went for lunch and that is when my mother told her about her horrible, incorrigible daughter. Shockingly, my aunt offered to take me home. My mother thought she was crazy. My mother told her not to waste her time because she would be kicking me out in six weeks so she should save herself the hassle. My aunt said she would like to give me a chance. Only God could have put that on her heart. My mother consented. I thank God for that precious lady, my dear auntie-mom.

Alice gave me an incredible home. She put me in painting classes at the University of Alberta, ballet, piano, guitar, and a summer drama school in Drumheller. Anything I was interested in Alice made a way for me to be able to do it. She proudly attended all my functions. She told me she was proud of me even when I pirouetted into a huge velvet curtain (which subsequently enveloped me) at a ballet recital.

The human psyche is such a mystery. Even though I was supremely happy living with my auntie mom I was a foul-mouthed brat. I would yell obscenities, stomp my feet, and slam doors. Thankfully Alice had a friend who was a social worker who advised her just to love me. If not for the wisdom of that lady, I probably would have become a ward of the government after all. I do not really know why I behaved like that. Alice said I had a hard wall around me that seemed impenetrable. I guess it must have been to guard my heart from further hurt. I think I was also subconsciously testing to see if I acted like a brat would I be kicked out. I probably wanted to be asked to leave sooner than later, before I became too attached to Alice and the beautiful life she was giving me.

Alice's kindness eventually won me over. I lived with her from Grades 9-12 and for three years of university. Alice worked as an internal auditor for Imperial Oil. Because I lived with her I qualified for an Imperial Oil scholarship and my entire university was paid for! What a gift from Alice, Imperial Oil and God! While I lived with her Alice divorced her husband George. He was an alcoholic and Alice was fed up with him. Bruce moved in a few years later when I was eighteen. He was the kindest, most considerate gentleman I have ever met. Alice treated me like the daughter she never had. She was the mother I never had. Bruce was like a dad. He told me I was like a daughter. Alice asked me to be the maid of honour at her wedding to Bruce Eaton. What an honour.

This is a side story but it demonstrates a powerful answer to a question I asked God. Alice and Bruce retired from Imperial Oil and moved to Tsawassen. I was visiting Alice at her home when I read a verse from the Bible that I found difficult to understand. Matthew 6:22 states, "If the light in you is darkness, how great is that darkness." That made no sense to me. I asked God to please show me sometime what that verse meant. That same day Alice and I went to a teahouse in Vancouver and I saw a woman that absolutely radiated light. I thought she must be an amazing Christian. I kind of forgot about the woman while Alice and I enjoyed our visit. After a while I glanced back at the woman to see if I could still see the light. I could. I was shocked to see she was holding someone's hand and was about to read their palm. She was a fortune teller. The verse "If the light in you is darkness, how great is that darkness" immediately came to mind. I realized the light in her was deep darkness. The Bible says even Satan himself can appear as an angel of light. I felt so sad for that woman but grateful God gave me such a graphic object lesson the same day I asked him a question.

I asked Jesus to be my Lord and Savior several times in my life, but the reality of a relationship with Christ didn't happen until I was in my early twenties. I desperately wanted Alice and Bruce to be in Heaven so I often spoke to them about God. At one point Alice said if I did not stop talking to her about God she didn't want to see me anymore. I told her I would miss her. Alice claimed she didn't need God. She said she had everything. Then, in what seemed like moments, almost everything was stripped away from her. She lost her precious husband Bruce, her ability to manage her own affairs, her health, was bed ridden for two years and eventually lost her life. Alice was completely under the care of others. She had paranoid dementia. It was really sad. Looking back I think she had early onset dementia for years. In her moments of clarity she cried and asked if this was all life was about. She complained and said she wanted the blonde caregiver fired who kept talking to her about Jesus. There was no blonde caregiver. The caregivers were from Africa and the Philippines. Two months before she died Alice prayed with me and asked Jesus to forgive her sins and be her Lord. I almost needed to pinch myself to make sure I wasn't dreaming. It was so surreal but very real. Alice also prayed with Lorna, one of the caregivers. Perhaps she prayed with the blonde caregiver also, the one I think was an angel. Lorna said Alice changed so much after she prayed. She became kinder and more thankful for everything. There was a new softness and gentleness about her. I am so thankful for the caregivers. They treated Alice like family. Lorna said she treated Alice like she would have treated her mother. I believe it was the love of these precious caregivers that helped soften Alice's heart and made it possible for her heart to turn towards God. I am so thankful this is not the end for Alice. She has really only begun to live. She is already in eternity in a place of infinite beauty, peace, love, and joy. I am so thankful.

My mother, Gloria "Ricky" Hunter, was in a horrible car accident in San Diego a few years ago. She was driving on a mountain road and the sun blinded her eyes so she didn't realize the road turned. She drove off a mountain cliff into a river. The emergency helicopter attendants declared her dead. Somehow, when she arrived at the hospital, she revived. She was in the hospital with a halo contraption screwed into her head for over a year. It must have been a brutal time for her. She never fully recovered. While in the hospital my mother prayed with me and asked Jesus to forgive her sins and be her

Rena Groot

Gloria "Ricky" Armstrong Taylor Hunter, my mother

Lord and Savior. She died shortly after being released from the hospital. My mother and my auntie-mom were never close. They now have eternity to have the relationship they never had on earth.

For the record, I have forgiven everyone who has ever hurt me. God has healed my heart so much I feel like I am telling you the story of someone else's life. However, I have a confession. I am sometimes envious of people who have lovely, Christian families. I wish I had a childhood full of the love, beauty and purity I see in the lives of others. The enemy of my soul likes to make me feel I have less to offer God right out of the starting blocks. It is easy to look at someone else's life and see beauty and wholeness. My life seems to have been so ugly and fragmented. I have often wondered how God could possibly use me. I really am happy for people who have had wonderful, happy lives. I do rejoice in the blessings of others. I have often wished I could have had that too. But, I trust God. I believe His ways are so much higher than mine and they are perfect. I trust and believe God will fulfill His plans for my life. I fully surrender everything to Him. I pray God will take the broken fragments of my life and multiply them exponentially to feed multitudes. I want a life that honours God and brings joy to His heart. I will need all of eternity to thank God that He rescued me. The cool part of this story is that God used Alice to rescue me and He used me to rescue her. I am forever grateful.

John

"There was a man sent from God whose name was John."
John 1:6

The Edmonton Militia advertised a Student Summer Employment Program (SSEP) that would give graduating students an amazing sounding summer. Students would be given a First Aid Course and be paid to learn and be certified. It sounded incredible. I joined the militia the summer before I began university. It was so much fun! We got to try out each Army unit for a week to see what was our best fit. The Medics Corps showed us gory films that made me faint (literally) so that was not my choice. The Royal Canadian Electrical and Mechanical Engineers flew us to Cold Lake to build a Bailey Bridge.

That was fun. We stayed at the Canadian Forces base for a weekend. The girls only got to carry metal spikes around and did not do any of the bridge building so they lost my vote.

There was a unit that repaired vehicles but I'm not especially mechanical so that was not my choice. Service Corps was a riot! I got to drive a deuce, a 2 ½ ton army truck and drove around an army base in an Armored Personnel Carrier (APC). I joined Service Corps and spent my weekends driving trucks during my first year of university with the Edmonton Militia. It was a blast!

That summer while driving a deuce around Canadian Forces Base Wainwright I got kind of lost in what I found out later was a simulated minefield area. A corporal suddenly stepped out of the bush and waved his arms at me to stop. He asked if he and his men could have a ride. They had been in the bush for days and were exhausted. It was perfect. They got a ride and I found my way back to the base. That was my first meeting with Hendrik Jan (John) Groot. We started dating when we were 18 and dated for two years. He was so sweet, except when he became moody, grumpy and mean. I knew I couldn't live with someone like that, that there was no future for us, so we broke up. We both desperately needed God.

There are years here I would rather leave out. I hate these puzzle pieces. When John and I broke up a week later another man asked me to marry him. I thought if I said "yes" I could tell John I was engaged and he would go away and find someone else. It was an evil, manipulative thought. I reasoned I could break up with this fiancé and then we could all live happily ever after. But John kept calling so I stayed engaged and the next thing I knew I was married to someone I barely knew. The marriage lasted six months. The groom was drunk out of his mind at the wedding. This takes you right to the window scene from chapter one, where I debated jumping.

Leviticus 16:2 says, "…for I will appear in the cloud above the mercy seat." Jesus had appeared to me in a cloud, sitting on what I thought was a throne. I realize now it was the mercy seat. That is where He had mercy on me and spoke life to me in place of death. How can I ever thank and praise Him enough? In the tabernacle in the wilderness the High Priest sprinkled the blood of the sacrifice on the mercy seat once a year on Yom Kippur, the Day of Atonement. The blood of Jesus, our Great High Priest, was sprinkled on the mercy seat for us. He made atonement for all our sin. What amazing love and mercy and grace He has lavished on us.

I left out part of what I felt God said to me until now because I didn't want you to throw this book into the garbage before you had a chance to hear my heart. What I also felt God say at that time was that I was to leave the relationship I was in. That did not make sense to me. I argued with God. I informed Him there is a verse in the Bible about what God puts together man should not pull apart. I have agonized over this next statement. Did I really hear from God? I heard Him say, "I did not put you together." I do not understand that statement any more than you do. I was 21 when I left the life that was killing me and began seriously searching for God. If I had stayed you would not be reading this book. The Bible says, "If you seek me, you will find me, if you search for me with all your heart." I was on a quest. God was the treasure I was searching for. My search took about two years. I finally found Him at a Charismatic prayer meeting and my life has not been the same since.

Shortly after I was "born again" and asked Jesus to forgive my sinful past and take control of my life, John started calling. I could not believe it. My first thoughts were, "God, please make him go away." I had no desire to ever see him again. John persisted in calling, so I began to wonder if perhaps God wanted me to talk to John and offer him a chance to be saved. I asked God to have John say yes to going to a prayer meeting with me if that was His will. I was positive this would be the end of John calling, as I was so sure he would say "no." The next time John called to invite me to his team's end of the year hockey party I told him I could not go because that was the same night as a prayer meeting I attended. John saw no problem with us doing both. So, we went to the Spirit-filled prayer meeting first. John hid in the bathroom for the worship service. When it seemed to have quietened down enough John came out and heard a message that hit him hard. I had no idea that he was mad at me after listening to the message. He thought I had informed the speaker all about his life. In all honesty I had never seen the speaker before and really had no idea what was going on in John's life. God was speaking to John.

Just a brief side note -- the prayer meeting I brought John to, which was part of the Catholic Charismatic Renewal movement, had a ten-week course called "Life in the Spirit." There was homework to do each week. I cried through the homework, asking God to cleanse me and make me someone useful for His Kingdom. At the last class all the participants were prayed for. One lady prayed for me and saw a picture of me as a lonely, beautiful flower blooming in a desolate place. That is why there is a lonely flower blooming on the back cover of this book.

After the prayer meeting we left for the hockey party. When I became a Christian everything became pure to me. I thought the people at the party were lovely. I had no idea people were hot knifing hash in the kitchen and that girls were offering to go home with John for the night. Later that night a stripper was supposed to jump out of a cake. I would have been horrified if I had known all this. What seemed like moments later

John came up to the table and said, "Come on. Let's get out of here. I can't handle this." I didn't understand why we had to leave. I did not realize the Holy Spirit was convicting John about the life he was living. His life was pretty much a mess. I had no idea what he was involved with. God's grace is the only reason John survived some of the situations he found himself in. One time while drunk and stoned he was driving his car at high speed down an icy highway and hit a school bus head on. The motor of his car was pushed into the seat beside him. He climbed out of that wreck with just a scratch over his eyebrow. But, that is his story.

A week later I had the joy of praying with John to receive Jesus as his Lord and Savior. I thought at that point my agreement with God for seeing John was over and God would have him move on. But he did not move on. He hung around and then about a year later started talking about marriage. Now that was a frightening topic. John persisted. My previous husband had committed adultery so I was free to remarry. Matthew 19:9 says, "And I say to you: whoever divorces his wife, except on sexual immorality, and marries another, commits adultery." Honestly, I agonized over this. Was adultery really grounds for divorce and remarriage? I did not want to make a mistake. I did not want to grieve God or disobey Him. I was advised by a pastor to call my ex-husband to see if he wanted to reconcile. I was overjoyed to hear him say he had found someone else. I was perfectly happy to remain single for the rest of my life. I had thoughts of going to China to become a missionary. I asked God to please show me His will. This was not going to be a casual asking. I had to hear from God.

It was Christmas 1979. I had two weeks holiday from teaching. I knelt by my bed and told God I had to hear from Him. I informed Him I was not going to eat or drink or move from that place until I heard from Him. I was desperate. I only wanted to do God's will. I believe when we get serious with God He gets serious with us. I fell asleep kneeling by my bed. At 3:00 am I woke up and "heard" God speaking to my heart. He spoke to me, not in an audible voice, but a voice I heard inside me that said, "Rena, marrying John will fulfill my highest purposes for both of your lives. It will be the hardest road you could possibly choose, but it will be the best one."

Even after hearing from God I still tried to dissuade John from marrying me. I was so afraid. My last relationship had brought me to the point of suicide, so I was petrified of marriage. I told John that because of weird hormonal stuff going on with me I did not think I could have children. If that was important to him he needed to marry someone else. I thought that would dissuade him. Around that time God gave John a vision of me walking on a beach with two little girls on either side of me and a baby girl in my arms.

Guess how many daughters we have? For some reason John did not see the boy. He was probably off exploring a tidepool.

I had John so worried about disobeying God he asked for a sign if marrying me was God's will. In the Bible Gideon asked God twice to confirm a decision he was making. John was driving his Triumph TR-6 British convertible sports car down the road on a Wednesday when he had the impulsive idea to say, "God, if this car sells by Saturday I will know it is Your will for me to marry Rena." That may sound like a strange request but that car was John's baby. There were no for sale signs on the car and it was not advertised. After John prayed that, at the very next light, someone yelled over at him, "Hey buddy. Wanna sell your car." They met at the parking lot of the next gas station. By the next day John had the money from the sale of his car and by Saturday I had an engagement ring.

Another piece of my life's puzzle was put in place when John and I were married on March 29, 1980. The theme of our wedding was "To God be the glory!" The life decisions we make obviously have a profound effect on our lives. The decision to marry John has probably brought me closer to God than any other path I could have chosen. There have been many times in our marriage I have cried out to God and informed Him that this is not what I signed up for. I told Him that He had been fair and warned me it would be the hardest road I could possibly choose, but He had neglected to tell me it would be this hard. I have also told Him I want all He has for me. I want to have the character He wants me to have. There have been times I have asked Him if I could please just settle for the amount of character I already have. He has not acknowledged that request. Maybe it is because I gave Him permission (as if He needs it!) to do whatever it takes to make me who He wants me to be. I informed God that if I kick and scream and complain just to ignore me. He has honoured that prayer. I praise Him for what He is doing in my life.

John had various jobs for the first several years of our marriage. He was ordained with the Pentecostal Holiness church in 1994. John worked as a lumber grader in Chilliwack for seven years. He was offered a foreman position at a new lumber mill but chose to be an operations manager at Circle Square Ranch in Manitoba and Alberta for two years instead. John was co-owner of Double Dutch Contracting in Stettler for three years with his friend Etienne Brugman. He was called to pastor Sundre Gospel Centre for five years. John resigned from his pastor's position in Sundre to become a full time student at the Canadian Southern Baptist Seminary in Cochrane. He earned his Bachelor of Christian Ministry and Master of Divinity degrees while simultaneously driving a school bus, working at a recycling plant, and being a paid on call firefighter/Chaplain. He worked on his Doctor of Ministry while pastoring in Penticton for two years. John completed a Doctor of Ministry in Spiritual Leadership and graduated from Golden Gate Seminary in San Francisco in 2014. He is currently on a Sabbatical from ministry and is driving a coach for Golden Arrow. This has taken him to camps in Northern Alberta in the winters and driving tour buses in the summers. This is one of the aspects of my life that I did not sign up for. We have mostly lived apart for the past nine years, but I am thankful to God for the opportunities this gave me to go on missions trips. If I had a 'normal' life you would probably not be reading this book. I am sure John is an encouragement to people wherever God leads him. I am thankful to have a husband who allows me to follow God's leading. He has whole-heartedly supported me in my many adventures. John has told me the final chapter of his life has not been written yet so I am waiting to see what God has planned for Hendrik Jan Groot. I am believing for wonderful things for him.

School

*"…that the God of our Lord Jesus Christ, the Father of glory,
may give to you the spirit of wisdom and revelation in the knowledge
of Him."*
Ephesians 2:17

It now seems like I was a student at the University of Alberta for moments instead of years. I graduated with a Bachelor of Education degree with a major in Special Education and a minor in Art. The photo is my graduation picture, autographed by baby Shalev Alice. I student taught at Sir Alexander Mackenzie School in St. Albert, Alberta my last year of university and was offered a teaching position at that school. The night before the Superintendent of the School Board called me with an offer I was at the Banff School of Fine Arts attempting to learn French and wondering what grade I would like to teach if

I had the opportunity to choose. I decided Grade Two would be the perfect grade. The children would be at an impressionable age and would need love and encouragement to give them a good foundation for learning. Guess what grade the Superintendent offered me? I loved teaching Grade Two. Honestly, I was so surprised to get a paycheck each month. I would gladly have taught for free.

While at Sir Alexander Mackenzie God put on my heart to start a weekly Bible study. This was in a public school. I decided there was no harm in asking the school board and the principal for their approval. My motto is "nothing ventured nothing gained." They both said "yes." I asked the principal for permission to use the library to show a film called "Sammy," the story of a paraplegic boy and how his faith in God brought his entire family to Christ. This was to be my introduction to the Bible study. The principal did not see the point of my using the Library. He thought my classroom would be large enough to hold all the students as he did not expect a big response. Surprisingly for him, over two hundred students showed up. I gave the students letters for their parents explaining what the study was going to be about (the life of Jesus) and asking them to sign a permission form for their child to attend every Monday at noon. That study ran for two years. I wonder how many lives God touched through it?

One day I was having quiet time in my classroom before school and read the verse, "Blessed are you when you are persecuted for righteousness sake, for yours is the kingdom of heaven" (Matthew 5:11). This might sound crazy but I asked God if I was doing something wrong because was there no persecution. I also asked Jesus to show me if I was to continue teaching at SAM or if I was released to join YWAM the following year. If the Bible study was allowed to continue I would stay for that. I then read, " Behold I have set before you an open door that no man can close" (Revelation 3:8). That Word sprang to life in my heart but I did not know why. That day the principal came to talk with me. He asked me to stop the Bible Study. I was so surprised. It was only December. The verse "I have set before you an open door" came to mind. I reminded him I had permission to have the study for the entire school year. He said that was true, but if I intended to teach at SAM the following year he would not give his permission for the Bible study to continue. I asked him why. He said other teachers were complaining. They did not like the fact that students were coming to me throughout the week for prayer about health or family or personal issues. It might sound a bit insane, but I actually rejoiced that I was being persecuted. It just happened to be behind my back so I had been unaware of it. God answered my questions the same day I asked them. I was being persecuted, I had an open door that year that no one could close, but the door was closed for the following school year so I was free to leave. Isn't God amazing?

One day I was so burdened as I imagined my fellow teachers standing before God unprepared to meet Him. I felt such compassion for them. I did not want any of them to be lost. I also did not want any of them to turn to me with accusing eyes and say, "You never warned us!" There were over forty teachers. I do not recommend doing this unless you believe God is telling you to. I am not completely certain this was His plan but one day I put a Gospel tract in each teacher's mailbox. I do not think that boosted my popularity. One teacher did ask me to explain to her about Jesus. I hope at least someone will be standing in Heaven because I was willing to look like a fool.

This is a beautiful message sent a few years ago from Janet Annesley, a precious former Grade Two student of mine from SAM (Sir Alexander Mackenzie). I have permission to share this with you.

Rena — can you believe it was 30 years ago! You did inspire in me my faith. I can clearly remember the feeling of you praying with the class, and although young, I felt something inside me move, a feeling of connectedness with the universe. In the following years, I developed my faith at church and through a wonderful summer camp near Caroline, Alberta. I still have so many lifelong friends from there! Aside from being a role model of spiritual teaching and giving, you were also a fantastic teacher and gave me considerable intellectual confidence at a very crucial time. Thanks be to God for putting you in my life, and I am sure the lives of so many others.

I have prayed over the years that you are well. It gives me great peace to know you and John are passionate about your family and what you do because you are both so good at it and the world needs you. So, thank you and thanks to God for making life so cool.

Much love,

Janet

P.S. Although your picture on the screen is very small, it is exactly the way I remember you! Very motivating for a grown woman like me to know that her childhood memories of a beautiful favorite teacher are real, not imaginary!

John and I were youth leaders at Elim Chapel, our little church in St. Albert. Our youth group decided it would be fun to put a float in the St. Albert rodeo parade. Our idea was the float would be covered in flowers with letters on the front that said, "Jesus said," the sides would say, "Behold I come quickly," and the back would ask, "Are you ready?" The youth group spent an entire night making plastic flowers. Do you have any idea what a blast it is hanging out with a group of giddy, sleep-deprived teenagers? If you have not tried it I recommend it. The youth group dressed as shepherds and handed out the tracts we made. The cover of the tracts asked, "Are you ready?" and inside there was a presentation of the gospel. The tracts were handed to people along the parade route. This next part is really cool. I thought it would be great to have a generator blasting out kids praise songs on the float with little angels bopping to the music. The problem was we did not have enough little angels in our church. I sent home a letter with my students asking parents if their child could be an angel on the rodeo float. There were only two children from my class who were away so missed being on the float. Over twenty little angels bopped past the judges stand to the music "Amen, praise the Lord!" from Kids Praise. They looked so adorable. We even won an award.

During the time I taught at SAM I lived in an apartment in St. Albert. One day I randomly decided I should sew an appliquéd banner for my church. The only problem was I did not have a sewing machine. I was about to haul all my sewing stuff over to my auntie-mom's house when I felt God say I should use a sewing machine in the building. I had no idea who had a sewing machine. I felt God suggest I walk through the halls with my sewing stuff and He would tell me when to stop. In case this really was God speaking I did not want to miss it. I decided nothing ventured, nothing gained. I walked through the halls with my sewing stuff until I felt God telling me to stop at the last door on the last floor.

I do not remember the lady's name so I will call her Jane. I had never met her before. Jane's guest room was also a sewing room. It was incredible. I was fasting that day but as I sewed Jane brought me cookies. I was going to ignore them but God told me not to offend her and eat them. He hates religiosity. After a few hours Jane came in with a stack of photo albums. She asked for my opinion. The albums were full of articles she had cut out of magazines and were things clairvoyants like Edgar Cayce and Jeannie Dixon had said regarding future events. I told her my opinion did not matter at all. What mattered was God's opinion. I asked her if I could tell her what He thought of fortune tellers. She was interested so I grabbed my Bible from my apartment and Jane and I had a Bible study. (Deuteronomy 18:9-14 warns people not to have anything to do with the occult.) I advised her to throw the photo albums in the garbage and trust in God. Now this next part was really incredible. A week later I was collecting my mail from the community mailbox in the apartment lobby when another resident asked if I had heard the news about Jane. I hadn't. Jane was dead. I was shocked. I realized God had given Jane time to repent and turn from the garbage before she stood before Him. I am so thankful I listened to His voice.

I have taught in several different schools: Sir Alexander Mackenzie in St. Albert, Highroad Academy in Chilliwack, Agassiz Christian in Agassiz, BC, Penticton Christian School, and Maple Leaf International School in Tianjin, China. While at Penticton Christian School Joyce Wiersma and I organized an end of the year beach party for our classes. At one point we called our students and asked them to line up along the beach for ice cream. I had one bucket of ice cream. As soon as they saw the ice cream every child on the beach lined up. There was not enough for all the children. I decided to just keep scooping and when I ran out I would just have to apologize. But I didn't run out. The last child waiting in line got the last scoop. God is so amazing.

A really cool field trip I took a few classes on from Penticton Christian School was an overnight trip to the Vancouver Aquarium. We had fundraisers to make money for our trip. The first part of our trip was a drive for five hours from Penticton to Vancouver to the Old Spaghetti Factory for dinner. One of the moms had sown cloth bags for us to put gifts in for homeless people. We put toothpaste, a toothbrush, soap, granola bars, a Bible, a water bottle, etc. into each bag. Each child had one bag to hand out. They prayed that God would be with the person they gave the bag to. We also brought along take away containers. When our dinners arrived at the Spaghetti Factory each child took half their meal and put it in their takeaway container for a homeless person. When we left the restaurant the children handed out the gift bags and dinners as we walked to our bus. I hope the memory of being a blessing stays with those children for life. Sleeping at the aquarium by the beluga whale tank was an amazing experience. The staff told us as long as the children were quiet they would leave the soft lights on in the tank so we could watch the whales. The silence was deafening.

John pastored in Sundre, Alberta for five years. While there the church sent us to a three day Billy Graham School of Evangelism Seminar in beautiful Lake Louise. All the attendees wore name tags to let others know our names and where we were from. The recurring question when people looked at our name tags was, "Sundre? Have you been to the Canadian Southern Baptist Seminary in Cochrane?" So many people asked us that we wondered if God was speaking to us. We stopped by the Seminary on our way home from Lake Louise and two months later John was enrolled as a student. The Seminary had a great offer for spouses. We could attend classes for half the usual tuition cost. I was homeschooling my children at that time so I decided it would be wonderful to be able to take a few classes so I did. Every semester. The last year John was at the Seminary I looked at the syllabus to see what classes I was interested in. I was so surprised to see if I went to school full time that year I would have all the requirements for a Masters degree.

Rena Groot

All the children went to public school that year and John and I graduated together with Masters degrees. So I have a Bachelor of Education degree and a Masters of Religious Education. I love how things, like a Masters degree, are not on my radar screen and they suddenly pop up and God seems to say, "Surprise!!" The next chapter describes a huge surprise blip on the radar screen that spanned several years.

Circle Square Ranch

"Come and hear, all you who fear God,
and I will declare what He has done for my soul."
Psalm 66:16

Have you noticed there are places on earth that will live inside you long after you have travelled on? Sometimes you will find yourself among unfamiliar faces only to discover you have found forever friends? Circle Square Ranch is one of those places. I saw an advertisement on a Christian TV program called 100 Huntley Street asking people to volunteer at one of their camps for a summer. There were ten ranches across Canada. The summer of 1981 John and I applied and were accepted as volunteers at Circle Square Ranch in Halkirk, Alberta.

Rena Groot

We did not have children at this time so we were free to be fully involved at "The Ranch." It was an incredible place. There was a Teepee Village for the younger campers with a petting zoo and playground. The older campers stayed at Western Town. It was the coolest place. The dorms looked like Old West storefronts. There was a Town Hall, Bakery, Coulee Laundry, Gunsmith, Wells Fargo, Express Post, Law Office, Bank. Whoever came up with the idea to build the ranches to look like an Old West Town had a genius idea.

A pony express rider rode in almost daily to deliver mail. The counsellors sent encouraging messages to their campers and each other by Pony Express. One summer, we celebrated "Happy Unbirthdays" among the staff daily. It was a challenge to find a gift to give each person. Sometimes we had secret friends and prayed secretly for a week for another staff member. It got kind of crazy. People were trying to "out bless" each other. One person gave their secret friend a $100 Bible. Another person gave their secret friend my stereo. Yes, you read that correctly. It was such a joyful, fun place to be!

Skit night was loved by all. Some of the skits were so hilarious we laughed until we cried. Mark Lefebvre's Martian skit was hysterically funny. Mark tried to fight the enemy in his own strength which, of course, came across as being impossible because Satan doesn't fight fair. John and I were famous for "The Heart Skit." It was a mime set to music. The skits started off funny, but slowly turned more serious. Some of the skits, like the "Heaven or Hell" skit the staff produced, probably inspired a lot of campers to choose to follow Jesus.

In the early years at the Halkirk Ranch we had problems (more like a crisis) with the water. The Ranch was built on the crest of a hill near a deep coulee (think small version of the Grand Canyon). That water issue was a surprising blessing. You are wondering how not being able to shower or wash your hair for a week could be a blessing? Well, there was a river close to the Ranch. On Saturday afternoons after the campers left, the staff went to the river. It was our communal bath place. Can you imagine how grateful we were for that river? I had the most wonderful smelling jojoba shampoo. Just imagine over twenty people standing in a river with jojoba smelling sudsy heads. Many people driving by understandably stared at us. There was a bridge there and some of the braver ones loved to demonstrate their courage by leaping off it. Such awesome memories.

One night during teen camp there were around one hundred people in the big teepee worshipping God. Someone began screaming. Their shrieking was actually louder than the one hundred singing voices combined. I looked to see where the sounds were coming from and was startled at what I saw. A young lady was screaming with a look of complete terror on her face. The weird thing is a face appeared to be hovering over her face. This is kind of hard to explain. I could see both faces, but the hovering face looked like a grotesque cat face. It had slanted eyes and fangs. I honestly thought I was seeing things. The director, Gary Lefebvre, motioned for me to take her out of the teepee. My thought was something like, "Are you crazy?" As the screamer and I left the teepee I grabbed a few other counsellors. We prayed together and then asked Rhonda if she wanted to be set free. A tiny, barely audible voice said, "Yes." John had a vision of Rhonda standing in a cage. He told us there were bars all around her but what she didn't realize was that the top was open. There was a way of escape. She only thought she was trapped. Rhonda told us she had been involved in the occult. Her grandmother had paid for her to come to the Ranch, hoping God would touch her heart there. I think Grandma must have been fasting and praying for Rhonda. She agreed to go, thinking she would like to cause chaos at the Ranch. We prayed and John said he saw the bars fall flat. God set that precious young lady free. The last we heard of her she had gone to Bible school. Her life was transformed. God is so amazing!

At one point I was asked to be on kitchen duty for a week. I asked God why. I grumbled as I stood at the sink watching campers and staff happily running by the window. I thought I should be with them. After all, I was a certified teacher. I had come to camp for the campers. Washing dishes was not what I had signed up for. God spoke to my heart then and the basic message was: "You have gone from teacher to dishwasher. I went from Lord of all Creation, seated on the throne of the Universe, to a helpless babe wrapped in rags in an animal's feeding trough." I apologized for my pride and complaining heart and asked Jesus to forgive me. All of a sudden washing dishes and being a servant to these precious people seemed like an amazing privilege.

Circle Square Ranch became a huge part of our lives. We had no idea that would be our summer for years to come. We loved it!!! All the staff were given quirky names, like Bambi (a beautiful girl with huge eyes)and Roper (who was famous for his calf-roping skills). Because John had longish hair and a beard it was decided that his name would be John the Baptist, or JB for short. When John the Baptist baptized Jesus a dove appeared, so it was decided my camp name would be Dove. After a few weeks people did not know anyone's real names anymore. I still get messages addressed to Dove.

At one point Bernie Doan, the new director, called and invited us to be on permanent staff in Halkirk, Alberta. This next part is quite surprising. This is not being told to you to be boastful, but to express my amazement that God made us such an integral part of the ranch. Bernie said he asked his children of all the staff that had ever been at the Ranch who did they think should be invited to be on permanent staff. Surprisingly, they unanimously said JB and Dove. We had just started leading the youth at our church in British Columbia when we were invited to be on staff so we sadly told Bernie it was not possible. After we said no we agonized over whether we had made a mistake. I remember lying in bed one night about a month later while John and I sadly discussed how we thought we had missed God. John called Bernie to say we would come after all. Unfortunately, Bernie had already called someone else and they had accepted. Bernie suggested we call 100 Huntley Street to see if any other Circle Square Ranches were looking for staff. The Manitoba Ranch invited us to fly out to meet their staff and to see if we would be a fit there. I was expecting a baby and almost was not allowed on the plane as it looked like I was due any moment. I had to phone my doctor and have him send a memo to the Vancouver airport that I was really only six months pregnant. We almost missed our flight. John told me later he felt God saying no about Manitoba but we were so desperate to serve God we said yes.

The puzzle pieces are all so connected. I have to pause the Ranch story to tell you about two of the most loving people I know. Fenn and Pier Riemersma are dairy farmers. Fenn is my husband's sister. They love God and have instilled a love for Him in their children. While we were at Circle Square Ranch in 1981 one of the volunteers in the kitchen told us she was so worried about her son. He needed to get away from his environment and find new friends. We called Fenn and Pier to ask if they would like another son. They said yes. Rob lived with them on their dairy farm for years. So, when we left Chilliwack in 1994 to move to Circle Square Ranch Manitoba, we had two little girls and I was nine months pregnant. My baby really was due any minute. Fenn and Pier found people to look after their farm and children while they were away and drove half way across Canada with us to be there if we needed help. Amazing people. I am so grateful to them for their kindness.

One of the members of the Board of Directors for Circle Square Ranch in Manitoba, Reverend John Howson, was the Director of Bridges for Peace Canada. He invited us to visit the Bridges for Peace offices in Winnipeg. This began a love affair with Bridges for Peace that has continued to this day. We stayed at Circle Square Ranch in Manitoba for six months, but our hearts were at the ranch in Halkirk. John called the director and Bernie said amazingly the Operations Manager position was open. We drove through a blizzard in November with our two little girls and our baby to get to

Halkirk. For the next two years John was so busy as the Ranch Operations Manager we barely saw him. One day Bernie sadly told us 100 Huntley Street was experiencing financial difficulties and he would have to let us go. We moved to Stettler and John began Double Dutch Contracting with Etienne Brugman, the Ranch's Program Director who was also asked to leave. The next puzzle pieces were being dropped into their places.

Chilliwack

"I am the vine, you are the branches.
He who abides in Me, and I in Him,
bears much fruit; for without Me you can do nothing."
John 15:5

"A spiritual kingdom lies all about us, enclosing us, embracing us, altogether within reach of our inner selves, waiting for us to recognize it. God Himself is here waiting for our response to His Presence. This eternal world will come alive to us the moment we begin to reckon on its reality."

-- A. W. Tozer

Our first summer at Circle Square Ranch was almost over. I was excited about going to Cambridge, Ontario, to a YWAM Fine Arts Discipleship Training School. Inexplicably, just before we were to leave on what I expected to be the adventure of a lifetime, John announced he did not feel we were supposed to go. That was a shock and a huge disappointment. We prayed and asked God to show us where He wanted us. The Ranch said we could stay and help them until we figured things out. John's sister from Chilliwack called at that time to say they needed a teacher at a Christian school her children attended. We assumed God was directing us so we moved to Chilliwack, British Columbia. That was a totally different kind of adventure from the one I anticipated.

We woke up the first night in our rental home thinking the train was coming through the house. We were that close to the train track. I found out that Margaret Bennett, the teacher I thought I was coming to replace, was only a few months pregnant and still working. I volunteered at the school but did not begin teaching full-time until about seven months later in the spring. While we were still at the Ranch, John thought he had work in Chilliwack. When we arrived he was told the construction company did not have work for him after all. I substitute taught at a high school and briefly worked at a restaurant to try to make ends meet. John could not find work. He was extremely discouraged. We moved into a more economical apartment (aka slum) but still found it difficult to make ends meet. When I did start work at the Christian school my pay was very meagre. It was under $1000 a month. When I inquired about a $100 a month raise John and I were advised to curb our lifestyle. John was not impresssed. It was a rough time. We burned through our savings for YWAM. One night at a prayer meeting we told three older couples about our troubles. They prayed for us and while they prayed they also stuffed money into John's shirt pocket. It was very humbling. I will always be thankful for the kindness those dear people showed.

We attended a church called Glad Tidings. They have since changed the name to City Life. A group from Glad Tidings met in our apartment on Friday nights to pray together before we went out street witnessing. One winter we stood singing songs and handing out tracts on the street near Five Corners in Chilliwack. (The photo for this chapter is of Five Corners.) Some teens across the road started making snowballs. These were not regular snowballs. They were packing rocks in them. I decided it would be a good time to hide out in a store. I was about to leave when I felt God saying, "Stand still and see the salvation of the Lord" (Exodus 14:3). I stood still and I am so thankful I did because I saw a miracle. The snowballs were coming directly at me and about half an arms length from me they veered off. It was wild! I could hardly believe what I saw.

One Friday night a man showed up at the street meeting who told us he was from far away. We asked where he was staying and he said by the railway tracks. Our church had just purchased land and there was a small house on the property. We asked if he would like to stay there if the pastor approved the idea and he said yes. There was such an authority about him. He seemed otherworldly. We took him to the house and left him a box of food. In a month he was gone. The box of food was still sitting untouched on the table. He probably would have preferred manna. I hear that is angel's food.

One summer John and I thought it would be cool to have a two-week vacation Bible school at our church. It turned out much better than anything I could have imagined. In the mornings we had a two-hour Kids Club. Dan Hamm was asked to build a small castle wall for people to hide behind to change costumes and for puppets to peek out from. Dan and Meda loaned us their beautiful puppets. Dan built a castle wall that could have been used in a medieval movie. It was unbelievable. He used plywood that had huge stones painted on it. The castle had turrets and windows. It was pretty amazing. John was the star of the daily Bible drama. He was a pilgrim searching for the armor of God and the fruit of the Spirit. There was a beautiful princess who was the narrator. I was the director. Baby Shalev had her first dramatic appearance as baby Jesus. We had so many amazing helpers.

The first week in the afternoons we had athletes from the Vancouver White Caps lead a two-hour soccer clinic. There were trophies at the end. Little Jimmy's Skate Club came up from Portland, Oregon to lead a one-week skateboard camp in the afternoons the second week. There were a lot of skateboarders in Chilliwack at that time. John and his friend Nico built ramps and Nico spray-painted his truck to haul the ramps around in. There was such a big turnout John and Nico decided to keep Little Jimmy's Skate Club going every weekend for a year. They received permission from the city to use a certain area for skating. Kids would come and half way through the skate time John and Nico would have the skaters sit on their boards while they shared a message about God with the skateboarders. It was pretty cool. From that two week Kids Club a neighbourhood Kids Club went on every weekend for two years. The first year it was held in Harold and Joan Hansen's garage. They were praising God when John's fiery object lesson went awry and the insurance paid for new carpets.

God did some amazing things in our lives while we lived in Chilliwack. I got a letter from my grandmother's lawyer saying the bank where my inheritance was being held in trust was closing. He asked if I wanted the money reinvested or if I would like to have it. Grandmother had put it in a ten-year trust fund because she felt if she gave it to me I would give all of it away. That was nonsense. I would have kept some. I asked my aunt and uncle if we could borrow $25,000 to be able to start building a house with the idea that when the money came from the inheritance I would pay them back. The day the money from my grandmother's estate arrived I called Alice and Bruce and asked if they would like us to go to their home to give them back their money. They lived about an hour and a half away. They said they would come visit us. When we applied for the mortgage on our house we had to tell the mortgage broker if we had any debts. We told him we owed $25,000. Bruce handed me an envelope. It contained a copy of the letter he had given to the banker. It said the money was a gift and was not subject to repayment. What a huge blessing! John finally found steady work. Chilliwack was really the best of times and the worst of times for us.

ywam

"But as many as received Him,
to them He gave the right to become children of God,
to those who believe in His Name."
John 1:12

A group from YWAM (Youth With a Mission) presented skits and testimonies at our little chapel in St. Albert. It was amazing! I was smitten. I had never seen anything quite like it and wanted to join YWAM more than anything I had ever wanted. John consented to go with YWAM for a year. I was ecstatic! I thought it was going to be as close to heaven on earth as you could get. I thought we would be with people who loved God and had a passion to make Him known. We almost went in 1981. For some reason God said no... or at lease John thought He did.

In 1984, after living in Chilliwack for a few years, God gave us the desire to take a year of our lives and pursue Him by going with YWAM. We wanted to know Him more and help others find Him. YWAM has bases all over the world so we had no idea where to apply. John had an interesting idea about how we were to determine where we were to go. He said we should pray about it for a month and at the end of the month we would write on a piece of paper where we believed God wanted us to go. I had the impression we were to go to Texas. Guess what John wrote on his paper? We had to check and see if there was a YWAM base in Texas. There was. It turned out to be the international base for North America.

We decided to sell everything we had. We did not think we were coming back. If it were not for the wisdom of our Pastor, Lorne Lueck, we would have had nothing. He suggested just on the off chance God had us come back to Chilliwack we should keep some of our "stuff." We sold our car, John's Harman Kardon stereo system, and most of our furniture. The Luecks kindly stored the rest of our stuff in their basement. Lorne said if we did not come back they would have a garage sale for us and send us the money.

We spent the summer at Circle Square Ranch and then flew to Texas in the fall of 1984. David Wilkerson had sold Twin Oaks Ranch to YWAM for $1.00 for every $100 the property was worth. It was a beautiful place. The DTS (Discipleship Training School) was a blessing. We learned so much about the heart of God for the world. We were asked to read great books such as Rees Howell's Intercessor, Bruchko, Peace Child, and Lords of the Earth. They were such inspiring books.

We had three months of classroom instruction and then about six weeks of outreach. The outreach options were printed on a corner of the chalkboard and we were given a month to pray about them to ask God to show us where He wanted us to go. The teams would then have a month to pray together, learn skits, and become a team. I informed the Lord that I was open to any option except the jungle of South Belize. I am not fond of snakes and scorpions. I advised the Lord that the North Belize team was my favourite option as they would be helping refugees. He was strangely silent. The night before we were to tell the leaders where we believed God wanted us to go I still had no idea where God wanted us. I was lying in bed discussing this problem with God. I told Him the next morning we must sign up for a team so could He please let me know where He wanted me. I waited. Finally I heard Him quietly say "Belize." I asked, "North or South?" And He said "South." I was in shock. I couldn't believe it. This was not what I had requested and was definitely not where I wanted to go. Why on earth would God send me to a jungle? The next morning I asked John if he had an idea where we were supposed to go. What do you think he said? Yup. Belize. Are you surprised? When I asked "North or South?" you will never guess what he said. You guessed it. He said "South." I felt like God and John were in a conspiracy against me.

We drove night and day in an old school bus for five days from Garden Valley, Texas through Mexico to get to Punta Gorda, Belize in a rather old school bus. Two drivers shared the driving. John had the night shift. I sat with him all night to keep him awake. John and I attempted to sleep during the day on the suitcases in the back of the bus. It was a rude awakening when we hit bumps. One night, in a small Mexican town, a policeman pulled us over. As he got on the bus he looked at his watch and then announced it was illegal to drive a bus down the main street between the hours of 2 and 4 AM. It was 3 AM so he arrested our bus. It was funny to watch the reactions of people as they woke in the morning to see a guard sitting by the bus on a park bench with a rifle across his lap watching us. We were summoned into the police station. The police wanted to be paid because they said we broke the law. YWAM Texas was called. Providentially, someone in YWAM Texas had a friend in that town who happened to be a dignitary. A few phone calls later and we were no longer being charged for traffic violations, but were being asked to pay for police protection. After all, a policeman had guarded us for hours through the night. He said it was a dangerous place for us to be. A few phone calls later and we were on our way out of the town with a police escort for our safety.

We dropped off the North Belize team and continued south. When we travelled as far south as you could go by land we were informed we would have to go by boats to Barranco. When we arrived at the dock I wondered where the boats were. There were just a bunch of logs in the water. We were told the dug-out logs were our boats. That was a bit unnerving. We had to travel across the Gulf of Honduras in these logs. I reminded God I couldn't swim, but told Him I trusted Him to keep us safe.

Do you remember me telling you I loved exploring tidepools when I was a little girl? Barranco was breathtakingly beautiful. The beach reminded me of my beach I explored as a tiny girl. There were conch shells and myriads of interesting things to see. The huts were almost right on the beach. The men went off fishing in the mornings then spent the rest of the day resting on hammocks. The women worked from sunrise to sunset. There was no electricity or running water so life there was very primitive. The majority of the people were children or elderly. Many of the 20-40 year olds had gone off to seek their fortunes in America. It seemed to me the children of Belize were mostly being raised by their grandparents. I visited the school one day.

There were about forty children with no books, no papers, no pencils. I did not really understand the purpose of them being there.

John and I stayed in a lean-to that was part of the chief of the village's home. For the village it was quite posh. There was a bed that had wooden slats and rolled up rags for a mattress. I praise God we brought a mosquito net. For some reason Belizean mosquitos ignored John but loved me. The room barely had space for a bed. There was no electricity so we had to do a room inspection each night with a flashlight. One night we discovered a massive spider trying to hide out in a corner. We knocked on the chief's door and asked if we could please borrow his big coffee can. It was his potty. In the mornings we heard the shutters open and then the squawking of poor unsuspecting chickens as he threw the contents of his can out the window on top of them. So, armed with the chief's pee can, John attempted to nab the spider. I had to follow the pursuit by flashlight. We hoped to capture the spider and release it outside the door. Unfortunately, John's aim was a bit off. I think he cut the poor spider in two. Surprisingly, especially for John, his arm was almost immediately covered with masses of tiny baby spiders. Perhaps it was inappropriate to laugh, but the look on John's face was priceless. The chief assured us later John was in no danger. Bites from that spider would only have paralyzed his vocal chords and made him unable to speak for a few days. No biggie.

One day there were no plans for the group so I decided to follow a jungle path to see where it led. I was armed with a machete and high boots, so what could possibly go wrong? Someone had introduced tigers to the jungle. Why they thought that was a good idea is beyond me. Thankfully this part of my story does not involve tigers or tommy goffs which are poisonous snakes so deadly that if you are bitten you have about a minute to get your life right with God before you stand before Him. I followed the path as it meandered through the jungle. It was incredibly beautiful. I am sure I was being led by the Holy Spirit because when I knocked on the door of a shack a weak voice invited me in. When I opened the door I was surprised to see no one in the room. The voice called again. There was a back room that could not be seen from the front of the house. A frail woman was lying on a bed. She looked like she was about to step into eternity at any moment. She had a huge greenish festering sore on her leg that appeared to be far beyond medical assistance. After greeting her I could not think of anything to say other than, "Are you ready to meet God?" It seemed like that meeting was imminent so there was no point of discussing anything else. The lady pointed to the ceiling to show me she was ready. Someone had placed a coffin in the open roof rafters above her head. It was so sad thinking that lady had to lie in bed and view her own coffin. She must have been full of fear. We talked about her spirit being ready to meet God and that dear lady prayed and asked Jesus to be her Savior. You will meet that precious lady in heaven one day.

This is a funny story. Belize used to be called British Honduras and there were British military bases still in operation. Our missions group met some British soldiers and somehow we were invited to the British Army base for dinner. They must have been desperate for company. After dinner we were asked to share our skits. We had some ice-breakers that were supposed to make people laugh. The soldiers stared at us with stony faces. It was a bit disconcerting. Gradually the skits became more serious. The more serious our skits became the more the soldiers laughed. When we presented a skit about what Jesus did for mankind the soldiers almost fell off their chairs laughing. The commanding officer must have noticed our bewildered expressions and ordered them to stop laughing. British humor is obviously very different from North American humor. A cool thing about our visit to that base is that a British doctor was able to cut the worms out of the bites of one of our team members. Don't you just love missionary stories?

We spent about a week in Punta Gorda with a missionary family from Nicaragua. Mrs. Anderson went to the market and led dinner home on a leash. She boiled the iguana in coconut milk and said it was called Belizean chicken. I did not want to offend my sweet hostess so I ate some iguana and fried plantain. It was surprisingly delicious. We also stayed at a YWAM base in Belmopan. That is when I really appreciated how amazingly easy life is in North America. I walked into the jungle to find a lemon tree and used a machete to get lemons for lemonade. At the end of our time in Belize, after about five weeks of adventures, we picked up the North Belize team and headed back to Texas. Do you remember how I had wanted to join the North Belize team helping refugees? I am so thankful God ignored my request and I obeyed His. That team spent six weeks digging outhouse holes. My recommendation is you listen to God. Do not insist on your own way. He wanted something far better for me. When we returned to the Texas base all the teams shared about their outreaches. John was our spokesperson. He did a great job of making all the other teams jealous. Ours was by far the coolest outreach.

After all the groups shared about their mission trips we were told we had to leave the base for six weeks until the School of Evangelism began. We had nowhere to go. We had spent all our money to come to Texas and take YWAM's training for a year. We had no idea leaving the base for six weeks was on the agenda. Someone suggested to us that perhaps we could be guest helpers at Last Days Ministries. While John and I were sitting at a fast food restaurant I was stressing about how we could contact Melody Green to ask about volunteering at Last Days Ministries for six weeks. John suggested I turn around.

The back of Melody's head was nearly touching mine. She kindly said we were welcome to be guest helpers. What a blessing.

While we were in YWAM we were privileged to be in an amazing area of ministry in Garden Valley near Lindale, Texas. Keith and Melody Green started Last Days Ministries to equip the church in her final days. The Last Days newsletters were sent out all over the world and had teachings to encourage believers. David Wilkerson had a ministry just down the road from our YWAM base called World Challenge helping drug addicts and alcoholics recover. David wrote a book about how his ministry began called The Cross and the Switchblade. It was a popular book that was made into a movie. There were many musical groups in Garden Valley when we were there. Dallas Holm and Praise, Silverwind, Second Chapter of Acts, Last Days Ministries and Agape Force were groups that helped shape Christian music in the eighties. Keith and Melody Green produced beautiful music. Rick Crawford, Dallas Holm's lead guitarist, was the worship leader at the house church we attended. It was an incredible blessing being in Garden Valley at that time.

While we were at Last Days Ministries Dan Cummings, our house church pastor, asked John to help him with a church he was overseeing. Dan preached at three churches every Sunday morning and was hoping John would help. John said he would love to, but God would have to provide a way for us to get there. We had gone to church every Sunday with our friends the Mannies but because the Discipleship Training School was over they had gone back to North Dakota with their car. We prayed about God providing a vehicle. John helped in the automotive shop with Carlos so he asked if he knew of anyone who had a car for sale. Carlos offered us his car for free. We asked him to pray about it for a week. What if he needed it? He prayed about it and a week later told us the car was ours. It was a Nova SS with an amazing pioneer stereo system. The car had never been sold. A car salesman had given it to missionaries in California who gave it to Carlos. When we returned to Canada we lived so close to our work we did not need it, so we gave it to Rhonda MacLellan who later gave it to the Vogts who were missionaries to Paraguay. It is amazing remembering these stories of God's faithfulness. I hope you are being encouraged to trust that we have a faithful God.

While at Last Days Ministries we began going to Leonard Ravenhill's Friday night meetings. Leonard Ravenhill was an English evangelist and author whose main emphasis was on revival and prayer. He challenged people to follow Christ uncompromisingly. People came by the busload from other states to hear him preach. He was an elderly, frail man who would slowly make his way to the podium. Once there it seemed the fire of God would hit him and he became a powerhouse. Once he had us stop singing "O for a thousand tongues to sing His praise" and exclaimed, "I thank God you don't have a thousand tongues! You can't even manage the one you have!" He said there was more fashion than compassion in the church. You get the idea. His messages made me repent every time I heard them. I asked Leonard a question about prayer after a meeting and I ended up being invited to visit him and his wife Martha for tea. John was also invited, but declined. I think he was intimidated by this fiery, passionate man of God. Leonard gave me a pile of amazing books about prayer and insisted I read them all. I'm sorry I did not ask him to autograph them.

In March 1985 we drove our new car back to YWAM for the School of Evangelism (SOE). People wondered why God blessed us so much. We wondered too. The main teaching for our SOE was "moral government" which was quite a controversial teaching that concerned us.

Our outreach for the SOE was to Metro Assembly of God in the ghetto in Brooklyn, New York City. Bill Wilson had a Sunday School of about 6000 children. About thirty school buses went out on Saturdays and Sundays collecting kids from all over Brooklyn. There were over 1000 in attendance at each of the five meetings. The drivers had to be sure not to collect kids from different areas as there could be gang warfare on the buses. Seriously. The church was in an old brewery. There was a huge fence around the compound with reams of razor barbwire on top of the fence. The week before we arrived the church was being fire bombed with Molotov cocktails. A huge Samoan with a sawed off shotgun walked the rooftop every night to be sure no one caused any problems. It seemed like we had arrived in a war zone. Bill told us that all the female workers had been raped. The week after we left someone left the compound gate open. One of the staff was working on his car in the compound and someone came in and kicked the jack over that held the car up. The staff member was crushed and died.

The Sunday schools were a one-hour extremely high energy program. The kids arrived to the sound of a band blasting out rock/praise music. Break-dancers danced in the aisles. There were contests and prizes. Bill presented a gospel message. The kids loved it. John coined the phrase "Sidewalk Sunday School" to describe the program we took to the streets. We had a mini bus that was painted with stars. The windows had curtains in them so puppets could be used at the windows. We put cardboard down on the sidewalks so kids could sit. Before the program began someone dressed in a Yogi bear costume strolled through the streets with a megaphone inviting kids to come. We had a half hour program that was always packed with kids and quite often very curious adults.

It was a blast. John was the team leader.

Everything went well until one day one of the team members asked if he could lead. I don't recall his name so I'll call him Fred. He was the same fellow who wanted to hire a prostitute so he could witness to her. We should have known better. It was like God removed His hand of protection and showed us what it was like without His covering. It was a nightmare. There was a kind of a magic trick that was used near the beginning of the program where a handkerchief was turned into a cane. Fred was doing the trick and said, "Eenie, meanie, minie mo, catch a nig...." We were horrified. Our audience was all black. The adults started grumbling. To make matters worse Fred threw the cane and it hit someone. Things started unravelling quickly. Someone climbed a tree and sat on a branch above us spitting on us. Part of the program was a contest to see who could drink a Coke the fastest, a boy or a girl. The girl threw up. That was the last straw. People started yelling and asking if the whites had come there to make fun of them. John called a halt to the program and we made a hasty retreat before things got even nastier.

One day the YWAM team leader's wife took me aside and asked me to stop giving my lunches away to the children that stood by the back door. I told her they were hungry and needed the food more than I did. She forbade me to give away any more of my food. God did something totally amazing then. There was a ministry in NYC that provided lunches for needy people. They had extras they didn't know what to do with so they donated them to Metro Assembly of God. Bill Wilson asked us to hand them out. Isn't God cool? The fridge and kitchen counters were full of food to give away. I didn't say anything, but in my heart I was laughing and rejoicing at God's sense of humor.

Bill asked John and I to stay and be part of his staff. We felt honoured to be asked. We prayed about it and agreed we would call the church back in Canada and see if they needed us. We decided that would be what we based our decision on. I had taught in their Christian school but my friend Margaret Bennet was teaching there while I was away. When we called I was quite surprised to hear that Margaret was pregnant (again) and yes they certainly did need us back!

We planned to live in Chilliwack for one year and then go back to NYC and help Bill and Kyle Wilson. Bill said he wanted a life commitment. I thought the way things were going there that really was not going to be that long of a commitment. As we drove from Texas back to Chilliwack we stopped by Circle Square Ranch in Halkirk, Alberta to say hello and show off our new car. They were delighted to see us. It was teen camp and they were short staffed. We spent a week at the Ranch then moved into Larry and Lorraine Balisky's guest barn in Chilliwack, BC. It was so much fun living by them. They often had missionaries over and we were invited to join them for visits and meals. Bill Wilson called quite often that year to encourage us about moving to NYC. He had to call the main house then Baliskys would tell us we had a call from NYC. Everything changed when we heard Kyle and baby Billy had left Bill. He could not give his family one day a week to just be a family. She wanted just one day to walk in the park and be a mom and dad with their little son. That is all Kyle asked for and Bill had refused. He said, "She didn't have the vision." I could see the possibility of that easily happening with John. We made a final decision not to go to NYC after we went to Europe for the summer. When we came home expecting baby Sarah we could not imagine bringing her up in the ghetto. God used YWAM to show me my focus should be on Him, not on what I thought would be an amazing ministry.

India

*"Most assuredly, I say to you, he who believes in Me,
the works that I do he will do also, and greater works than these he will do,
because I go to My Father."*
John 14:12

This is really John's story but I had a starring role in making it happen so I have to tell you about it. John and I lived in a little "guest-barn" in Dr. Larry and Lorraine Balisky's back yard in Chilliwack, BC. We saved up $3000 and were hoping to use it to as a down payment for our first house. So, one Friday afternoon we visited a builder to find out how much it would cost to have a house built. John had a hockey game with a church league that night so we did not have time to go home for supper. We decided to stop by a restaurant. As we walked by the restaurant window some friends who were seated inside started frantically waving at us to join them. Harold Hansen excitedly told us he was going to India in one week to help an evangelist with crusades. He turned to John and asked, "Why don't you come with us?" John laughed, but for some reason that question grabbed me and wouldn't let go.

As we drove to the hockey arena that evening, I told John I thought he should go to India. He protested and said he had not heard from God and we did not have enough money anyway. Harold said John needed $4000 to go. We only had $3000. After the hockey game, as we walked in the door, the phone started ringing. John's dad was on his way back from Holland and had stopped to visit his daughter Evelyn in Edmonton. Evelyn had told him we were hoping to build a house.

Now, before I tell you about the call, so you can appreciate how amazing this is, John's dad did not want us to go to YWAM the year before. He wondered why we couldn't be normal, just buy a house, settle down, and start a family. John's parents thought we were crazy! So, when John answered the phone and his dad said, "I hear you are buying a house" John expected his dad to be excited by the news. He was totally unprepared for his dad's reply. He said, "Don't do it! God has work for you!" That Sunday at church Harold came up to John and asked what he had decided. John said, "I'm going." Harold replied, "Good, we've already booked your tickets." The next morning the team drove a few hours to the Indian consulate in Vancouver to get visas. We were still short $1000. Harold's wife Joan called at morning recess at Highroad Academy, the school where I taught, to tell me someone had given her a check for John for $1,500. If John had decided not to go she was instructed to rip up the check and never tell us about it.

While in India John led worship one evening at a mass crusade. People lined up afterwards to see the evangelist for prayer. John was standing apart from the crowd. He said a small boy on crutches came hobbling towards him. The translator said the boy wanted John to pray for him. John was actually quite a skeptic about modern day miracles. The boy's feet were upside down and kind of backwards. John tried to redirect the boy towards the evangelist and the healing line. The interpreter insisted the boy wanted John to pray for him. The boy refused to leave. John told me later he had no faith for a miracle. He prayed something like, "God, you see this boy's faith. Please heal him." While he prayed John was shocked to see the boy's feet turn. The new tops of his feet were now covered with calluses. John said the boy gingerly took a few steps, then dropped his crutches and joyfully ran. Somewhere there's a picture of John with tears streaming down his face standing beside a crutch-less boy. I wonder what became of the boy? I am sure he will never forget what God did for him.

Europe

"For I know the thoughts that I think toward you, says the Lord, thoughts of peace and not of evil, to give you a future and a hope."
Jeremiah 29:11

Sharing the things God has led me to do for His Kingdom feels awkward. I am not trying to make you think great thoughts about me. My purpose is not to exalt myself, but to exalt God. He is the One Who deserves all glory and honor. I fully realize that any good in me is because of His goodness in me. I really can do nothing without Him. Okay, now that we have that bit of information out of the way, I can tell you more cool things God has done.

Rena Groot

John's cousin, Dirk Jan Groot, started an organization in Holland called Dorcas Aid. This is a ministry that takes food and clothing to persecuted Christians and Jews throughout the world. Dirk Jan invited John and I to spend the summer of 1986 with his ministry in the Netherlands in the hope we would start a Dorcas branch in Canada. Their current motto is "We strive for lasting change for those who live in poverty, are excluded, or are caught in crisis." In 1996 their motto was "Together we can make a difference." Dirk Jan asked us to make two trips with supplies behind the Iron Curtain. He wanted us to take food and clothing to people who had been affected by the Chernobyl nuclear disaster.

Dorcas Aid in Holland sent out a monthly newsletter to inform people of its work and of humanitarian violations. I have to tell you a story about Irina Ratushinskaya. It is a special story. Irina was a young Russian Soviet dissident, Christian poet and writer. She was imprisoned because of her outspoken beliefs. When I read about Irina in the Dorcas newsletter I wondered what it must be like for her in a Soviet prison. I wondered if she had a blanket to keep warm. I prayed God would comfort and encourage her, would hold her close and His arms would feel like a warm blanket around her. I prayed she would sense His Presence. This is the amazing part. Years later I read a news report that Irina had been released from the Soviet prison. She was asked what it was like in prison. Her answer made me cry. She replied almost word for word what God had put on my heart to pray for her. While in a cold Soviet prison she had felt God's Presence like a warm blanket wrapped around her. God is so awesome!

Our dear friends, Dan and Meda Hamm from Chilliwack, joined us on our Dorcas Aid trip to Poland. Dan felt God tell him to bring blue jeans along to give away. Somehow we ended up at a farmhouse. The papa in the house was exactly the size for the jeans and needed them. Small groups of us at a time were taken from the farmhouse to a deserted looking stretch of highway and dropped off. We followed the papa through the woods to a place where there was a surprisingly large group gathered to watch a secret river baptism. Two young soldiers were dedicating their lives to Christ. They realized that if their faith was discovered it would be the end of their military careers. They were risking all to stand for Christ. We met a Jewish man at the baptism and John gave him the Star of David necklace he had been wearing.

As I mentioned, this trip was right after the nuclear disaster at Chernobyl. Apples were falling off the trees before they were ripe due to the radioactivity. The people were hungry so were eating them anyway. It was a difficult time. We went into a store that had shelves stacked with food on display behind the front window. When we walked in the store all the shelves were empty except for the shelves by the window. We walked through the store and at the back was a glass case with some meat for sale. A butcher stood there so we motioned that we would like to buy a ring of farmer's sausage. He put out his hand so I assumed he wanted money. I tried to give him money, but he brushed it aside and showed me a ticket. The food was being rationed and we needed a ticket to buy anything. Of course we did not have a ticket. I watched the lady in the line behind me to see what would happen. The lady handed over a ticket and was given a piece of garlic sausage that was about two inches long. I felt so ashamed. We had tried to buy the whole sausage ring.

We arrived at Checkpoint Charlie in Berlin to leave Eastern Germany at around 3:00 am. If you have never seen the place it was quite intimidating. There was a huge raised platform with a tank on top of it. The turret of the tank pointed right at any vehicle stopping at the border. Our guard that evening was not happy. Maybe his wife burned his toast. He held up Dan's passport to his face and then squinted as he peered over it to stare at Dan. Unfortunately, Dan had a beard on his passport photo and decided to shave before the trip. Not a good plan. The guard's behavior was so peculiar I couldn't help but laugh. That did not amuse the guard. He gruffly told us, "So, you sink zis is funny? Go to ze back of the line!" Another guard walked towards us with a tool kit. He obviously was told to thoroughly investigate us. We had something he found interesting so we gave it to him. That was enough for him so his investigation concluded and we drove back to Holland without any further incidents.

Our trip to Romania was quite different. John and I went alone with a large panelled Volkswagen van full of supplies. We had purchased visas for three days. Dirk Jan had said that was how long it would take for all the drop offs. We arrived at the Romanian border at 5:00 am and thought we had lots of time to make drop offs. The border guards were suspicious of our van full of stuff so decided to detain us for twelve hours.

Nicolae Ceauescu was the leader of Romania at that time. Contact with the West was discouraged. Just for your information, Ceauescu was arrested in 1989 and tried by a military tribunal for his crimes against the people of Romania. He destroyed their culture, demolishing art galleries and museums. He tried to eradicate all traces of Romanian history. He moved people off their family farms, destroyed their homes, and squashed them into sterile apartment blocks in cities. Meanwhile, to no ones surprise, he and his wife lived in complete opulence. He and his wife were sentenced to death and shot.

So, meanwhile, back at the border crossing, we were asked to park the van and a man with a toolbox arrived. He climbed in the back of the van armed with a screw-driver and started to unscrew the panels. At one point he turned and barked, "Bibles. You have Bibles?" Dirk Jan told us not to take Bibles. He said we were too naïve and would get into trouble and possibly thrown into jail. I stood there feeling ecstatic that the guard thought we had Bibles. I thought this man obviously saw the love of God in us. I truthfully told him no. Moments later the guard turned and sternly demanded, "Porno! You have sexy porno?" The Bible says pride comes before a fall. I felt so deflated as I also truthfully told him we had no sexy porno.

Twelve hours later we were allowed to proceed. One of the guards called us greedy capitalists. He thought we were greedy carrying so much food and provisions for our-selves. We had told them we had so much stuff because we did not know what we would need for our trip across Europe. Our first visa day was used up at the border. Because we had only two days of visas left for three days of traveling we were understandably stressed. We were tired, hungry, and cranky. I remember lying in the back of the van on day three crying and telling God this was beyond my ability to endure. I was exhausted and did not realize it but I was expecting baby Sarah. My hormones were whacked. I was annoyed with John and decided when we got back to Canada it was all over between us. The spiritual warfare against us was intense. Somehow God enabled us to make all our drop offs with our marriage intact. The last drop off was the most dangerous.

We stopped in Timisoara, the city from which my great grandmother, grand-mother, and auntie-mom had all immigrated to Canada. We stopped at a grand ho-tel and decided to have dinner there. There were no lights, just candles everywhere. I thought it was so romantic. I didn't realize it was because they had no power. There was a huge menu written in Romanian and French. Thankfully my French was good enough to order food. The waiter kindly told us everything we tried to order was not available today. I finally asked what was available and from the huge menu there were two options, chicken or veal. We went through the same thing with the large salad menu just to find out there was one option, a cucumber salad. We ordered that. A moment later a sliced dill pickle was placed on our table. That was the cucumber salad. In another moment the two dinners arrived. John marvelled at how quickly we were served. He did not see what I saw. Behind him was a long table with chafing dishes on it. The dinners were being kept hot by candles under the chafing dishes. We found out later the people were given two hours of electricity each day so the meals were prepared then. The hotel rooms were way out of our budget so we slept on top of piles of clothes in the van.

I had written all the addresses in a secret code, backwards. So 123 became 321. Genius, right? So much for my espionage skills. I felt like I was working for the Department of Eternal Affairs so I wanted an element of mystery and intrigue. Our last stop was at a church where the pastor spoke no English and we of course spoke no Romanian. Thankfully, we spoke the common language of love. We showed the pastor the piles of food and clothes in the van and he somehow communicated that it was too dangerous to move everything in the daylight. It would have to wait until dark. Then he seemed to have second thoughts, somehow communicated that our God is big, and decided we would go ahead and empty the van in the daylight. I climbed into the back of the van and it seemed like people appeared out of nowhere to form a line of people from the van to the church. I passed stuff out until the van was empty. John asked if I got everything and I confidently said yes. We went into the church to pray with our brother. We just got inside the church when the police drove by. If we had still been dropping off stuff we could have all been arrested. John and the pastor hugged each other and cried on each other's shoulders. As we drove down the road John asked me if I had cleaned out the various areas where stuff was stored. I was kind of annoyed and wondered if he thought I was an idiot because I had already told him I had emptied the van. Then he asked about the wheel wells. Ah... THOSE wheel wells. I totally forgot about them. If I had remembered things were stored in the wheel wells we would have still been there when the police drove by. God protected us by having me forget to unload everything.

After we made that final drop off we headed for the border. We only had a few hours to be out of the country before the visa expired. No pressure. We did not know what to do with the wheel well stuff until God gave me a brilliant plan. I made care packages with the stuff and wrote messages on the bags like "God bless you!!!" and " Jesus loves you!!!" John asked what was the point of writing messages the people could not read. I told Him I thought the people would be curious and would hang onto the bags until someone could read them. It was hilarious seeing the startled expressions on people's faces as we pulled over the van, I hopped out, smiled and handed them a package, jumped back in the van and we sped off.

This next situation could have had a scary ending, but thankfully God protected us. At the time we had no idea how much danger we were in. Dirk Jan had told us that entire Christian families in Romania were being arrested and forced into labor camps. As we drove along I noticed a hillside full of men, women and children. They were all wearing the same clothes and seemed to be picking rocks. This may sound odd, but there seemed to be a glow about the people. Then I noticed the guards with rifles standing among them. I thought this verified Dirk's statement about arrested families so I decided to take a photo for his newsletter. I thought there was really nothing the guards could do as we were driving past and they could not stop us. However, about a mile down the road there was a barricade across he road. We had no choice but to turn around and drive back. I am sure you are not at all surprised when I tell you there were guards with rifles standing on the road waiting for us.

Have you heard of Richard Wurmbrand? He was a pastor in Romania who said Christianity and Communism were not compatible. Because of his statements he was imprisoned and tortured in a Romanian prison for fourteen years. At one point his feet were beaten so badly you could see the bones. Upon his release Richard started the ministry called Voice of the Martyrs. If I had thought at that moment about what had happened to him in a Romanian prison I might have been nervous. Thankfully, when scary things happen around me God seems to make this "bold as a lion spirit" rise up in me. Such mercy!

So a gun-toting guard walked up to the van. His face was serious and stern as he demanded "Photo! Photo!" I had dropped the camera on the floor of the van and covered it with my sweater. I acted like this was the most normal conversation the guard and I were having as I took pictures out of my purse to show him. He started miming taking a picture with a camera and getting louder with his "Photo!Photo!" demand. Finally in exasperation he called another guard who also went through the same "Photo! Photo!" routine. Finally the first guard in frustration gruffly told us to "Pass!" I wonder how far down the road we were when it dawned on him he could have asked us to get out of the van. We could easily have been invited to join the group on the hillside and I would be writing this in Romanian now.

We quickly realized God did not want us to pursue leading a Canadian office for Dorcas Aid. Dirk Jan wanted John to organize meetings across Canada and fly out to these meetings. We did not have the money to finance that and we certainly did not want the money people donated to help others go towards plane tickets. I don't think Dirk Jan had the concept of how big Canada is. As the Dorcas Aid door closed God opened a very different door.

Children

"Children are a heritage of the Lord,
the fruit of the womb is His reward. "
Psalm 127:3

The puzzle pieces are so interconnected the lines between the chapters are blurred at times. The details in this chapter are included with my children's permission. If it seems like there is more information on some children it is because they approved more. (Haha.) This is a picture of Shane, Shalev, Savannah and Sarah in 1998 when we lived in Stettler, Alberta. Do you remember the part of the story where God showed John a vision of three daughters? That was pretty much impossible, but God is faithful. We have three daughters and a son. They are all gifts from God.

I believe at the moment of conception our human, eternal, God-given spirit is infused into our tiny self and our spirit knows if we are wanted or not. Our children were all very wanted. John and I asked God for nearly seven years for our first child. While we were in YWAM in Texas we were invited to be helpers at a Bible camp for a weekend. We were told great food would be the pay. The bus quickly filled up. In YWAM the food was sparse. A large bowl of soup at lunch usually didn't make it all the way around each table. The food was from the food bank and was often out-dated. I am not complaining, I am just saying why the bus was full of eager volunteers. The first night after helping in the camp kitchen the group decided to hang out and watch a movie together. I was about to join my fellow YWAMers when I felt the Lord impress on my heart not to go with the group, but to stay and spend time with Him. I stayed behind. As I read "God is a rewarder of those who diligently seek Him" (Hebrews 11:6) I felt the Lord stop me and ask how I wanted to be rewarded. I was taken aback. I didn't feel like a diligent seeker. I felt God ask me to look up Psalm 127:3. I was surprised to read, "Children are a heritage of the Lord, the fruit of the womb is His reward." That was incredibly special. God spoke to my heart that we were going to have a baby girl and we were to name her Sarah Beth Groot. The initials SBG would stand for Sent by God. Guess what our first child's name is?

I had a pituitary tumor which caused chaos in my hormones. My pituitary gland (which is at the base of your optic nerve by your brain) over-produced prolactin so for ten years my body was tricked into thinking I was nursing a baby. I did not have a monthly cycle. To have a child was pretty much physically impossible. When we arrived back in Canada from Texas God led me to an endocrinologist who performed fibre optic surgery (through my nose) to remove the tumour and prescribed a drug called bromocriptine. (It sounds like something Superman would take). He said it would suppress the prolactin and I should be able to get pregnant. The strange thing is bromocriptine is the drug my mother told me she took when she was pregnant with me so her milk would dry up and she would not have to nurse me. Interesting, right?

So many people rejoiced with us when we found out we were expecting a baby. We were blessed with baby Sarah Beth in 1987. Sarah means "Princess." Beth means "house." Sarah was a very loving, sweet child. When Sarah was almost two we thought it would be wonderful to have another child partially so Sarah would not have to grow up alone. I had a random thought when I was expecting my next baby that if God gave me a little girl on Valentine's Day I would never doubt that He loves me. I was surprised at that and told God that thought was not from me. I informed Him I had no clue where that idea came from. Our baby was due the end of January. Guess what date Shalev Alice Groot was born? February 14, 1990. Just before our baby was born we went to a Passover Seder in Vancouver and John ran into a friend from Israel. We asked him about popular names in Israel. He said Shalev meant serenity. We thought it was a beautiful name so chose that for our baby. John's friend forgot to tell us one important detail. Shalev is a boy's name. Shalev's second name is Alice after her Grandma Alice. Alice means "nobility." Shalev is a unique, compassionate, free spirit kind of a person. She has a diploma in Criminal and Social Justice because she had plans to right the wrongs in this world. I think she realized what a formidable task that would be so all future options are open. I am sure Shalev will do well in whatever she aspires to.

In 1992 we were excited to find out we were expecting a third baby. I asked God what her name was to be. John had a vision of three girls so I was sure this baby must be a girl. I felt God said her name was Aliyah. Aliyah had not even taken her first breath when she went to meet Jesus. I found out afterwards that the Hebrew word "aliyah" means to ascend or go up. I was devastated. I asked God to comfort my heart and I was pretty much immediately filled with His peace until that spring around the time she would have been born. As I was walking through a grocery store I saw a lady walking by with a newborn in a baby buggy. I burst out crying. Losing Aliyah made my children even more precious and gave me more compassion for others who have lost children.

When John and I were in Israel with Volunteers for Israel (Sar El) we visited Yad Vashem, the Holocaust memorial. Many of us stood around weeping after walking through Yad Vashem's Children's Memorial. Allouche, our "Madrich" (leader) challenged our group and said, "If you have finished having your family, have one more to replace a child lost in the Holocaust. "A year later in 1994 we sent him Shane Michael Bruce Groot's birth announcement. Allouche sent us a beautiful "Mazel Tov!" (Congratulations!) card from Israel.

Shane means "a gift from God," Michael is the name of the angel that guards Israel (Daniel 12:1), and Bruce means "strong and brave." This name was given in honor of Grandpa Bruce. When Shane was about a year and a half he was sitting on my lap facing a lady who was tearfully telling me about her miserable marriage. Shane was intently watching the lady and sucking feverishly on his soother. He seemed to be really concerned that the lady was upset. Finally, almost in an act of desperation, he took his precious soother out of his mouth and offered it to the lady. He was just a little guy with a huge heart, wanting to bring comfort to an obviously distraught lady. It helped. It made her burst out laughing. Shane was the most adored baby at the Ranch. As a little two year old he got to ride around with the staff in trucks and on tractors. He hardly walked anywhere because someone always wanted to carry him. He loved it.

I kept a journal for each of my babies. This is an excerpt from Shane's journal.

> Dear Baby,
> Hello precious child. God started you a month ago. Your family, daddy, mommy, Sarah and Shalev have been praying that God would bless us with a baby. We are so thankful to God for giving you to our family. Psalm 139:16 says, "You saw me before I was born and scheduled each day of my life before I began to breathe. Every day was recorded in your book."

One day, when Shane was about three years old, I heard him calling, "Help! Somebody help the boy!" He had climbed up the outside of the staircase in the yard and was hanging on the outside of the patio railing. I asked what the problem was and Shane said he didn't know how to get down. I thought this was a great teachable moment so I told him when you are not sure what to do you should ask God to help you. He said something like, "God, help the boy." I thought I could be the answer to his prayer so I suggested he climb down the same way he got up. That seemed like a great idea to Shane so he climbed down the outside of the stairs and was about to run off. I told him when God helps you then you need to thank Him. Shane called out, "Thanks God. Bye for now." Shane loved BMX biking and as a young boy spent a week at Circle Square Ranch in their BMX program. As an adult he took a three-month intensive fire-fighters course and is now an auxiliary firefighter in Penticton. If there was an emergency Shane would be a great person to have around, as the crazier things are, the calmer Shane gets. He also works for Telus selling cell phones and is their top salesman. The following story highlights his humor. Once upon a time Shane had his X Box confiscated by his very wise mother because his room was a disaster. It was to be returned once his room was cleaned. After the clean-up Shane appeared looking like Moses wearing a towel beard, draped in robes made from sheets, holding a hockey stick like a staff, demanding, "Let my X Box go!" It was hilarious. He has such a great sense of humor.

While we lived at Circle Square Ranch in Halkirk, Alberta, little Sarah and Shalev started praying every night for a baby sister. Shane was only two so did not join in on the prayer. God heard them. Savannah Evelyn was born in 1996. She has complained about her name because Savannah means "a grassy field" and she thinks her siblings have cooler meanings for their names. Sharon, a friend I met in Israel who is from South Africa, said if she could ever see how beautiful the savannah is she would be honored to have that name. Evelyn means "beauty or radiance." In Irish it means "hazelnut." We won't go there. Savannah pursued Air Cadets (where she earned almost every award available), modelling, acting, voice lessons, and serving at Earls and Cactus Club. Savannah broke her collarbone twice. She went to an Air Cadet weekend at Apex ski resort. While sitting on the side of the hill with friends another cadet skied into her back. It is a miracle the accident was not worse. She suffered a herniated disk and after two years of pain and morphine had back surgery. She went to Thompson Rivers University and tried valiantly but was unable to continue her studies but could not concentrate because she was on morphine for pain. Savannah weaned herself off the morphine and is currently contemplating getting an Arts Degree and then either going into medicine or getting an Education Degree to become a high school Drama, English, or Math teacher. Another idea she is considering is getting a business degree and helping a friend who is a chef start a restaurant. So many options. She went to Israel on a Birthright trip. This is from their website. "Taglit-Birthright Israel (Hebrew: תגלית), also known as Birthright Israel or simply Birthright, is a not-for-profit educational organization that sponsors free ten-day heritage trips to Israel for young adults of Jewish heritage, aged 18–32." Their goal is to have young people see the land and fall in love with it and want to move there to build it. Their plan seems to be quite successful. Savannah has mentioned the possibility of being a lone soldier in Israel. A lone soldier has left their family in another country and gone to Israel to serve in the IDF (Israeli Defense Force). Savannah spent twelve hours on the plane flying to Israel learning the Hebrew alphabet from a lady who sat beside her. She sent a message from Israel and said she had been set up with the lady's nephew in Israel, so if we did not hear back from her again she was probably traded for several camels and a donkey. If she wanted to she could easily become the Prime Minister one day. She is a very determined young woman.

We homeschooled for a number of years for a variety of reasons. The main reasons were because John and I thought homeschool would be the best way for our children to have a God-centred curriculum and avoid the peer pressure in school. They would also have time to develop their unique gifts and abilities as they had ample time for practising their musical instruments, baking, gardening and pursuing other interests. Sarah had her first job at the age of 11 watering plants at a greenhouse. Sarah and Shalev helped tend our huge garden in Stettler and sold heirloom sunflowers, vegetables and homemade bread at the local farmers market. It was their business venture. At 13, Sarah volunteered in a bakery/café where she learned how to make cheesecakes and pies. Shalev worked in a coffee shop. Sarah and Shalev were members of a 4H club and contributed their baking to club and church events. They learned how to sew and made pillowcases for homeless people. The girls all had ballet, jazz and piano lessons.

When we lived at the Seminary all four children lived in one small room on two bunk beds so our third bedroom could be a music room. Sarah had a Phantom keyboard and Shalev had electric drums. I thought their music was beautiful. Shalev loved gymnastics so was enrolled in gymnastics lessons. Shalev and Shane had golf lessons. Sarah and Shalev were campers at Circle Square Ranch and then took the Ranch's Leadership Training Course. Shane was on hockey teams when he was five and again as a young teen. Shane took violin lessons for a year. Sarah and Shalev had horseback riding lessons. When we lived in Sundre, Sarah and Shalev organized a week-long summer camp and named it Camp Cornerstone. I think they had three campers. I was the designated camp cook. All four children had swimming lessons. Sarah made it all the way to Lifeguard. Shalev got her Bronze Cross, Shane earned Bronze Medallion, and Savannah can swim. When we lived at the Seminary all the Seminary kids created a civilization named Burma. It became a very interesting kind of a civilization with their own money system and government. We found out later that it evolved into a *Lord of the Flies* kind of society. Thankfully it fell apart. Because we homeschooled we had money from the school board to purchase curriculum to use for music, swimming, gymnastics, art or Physical Education lessons. I think homeschool brought my children closer and enhanced their creativity. They weren't stamped out of a cookie cutter.

Shalev went to public school in Grade 12. I don't advise sending your child to school in Grade 12. It was traumatic and a culture shock for her. Shane went to a Christian school in Grade 10 and Savannah went in Grade 5. I personally believe, because of the way society is going, you are wise to keep your babies close. Just ask God to lead you. He will show you what is best for your family. In spite of the apparent good homeschool achieved in my family, I made a decision I thought was best but has since appeared to be a poor decision. I decided to have Sarah not get a government high school diploma. I somehow was under the impression homeschool diploma would be recognised by universities. I felt the public school curriculum that was offered my children was boring. The Language Arts program was dark and seemed like it was written for morons. I wanted my children to read classical writings and be inspired by great writers of great stories. We used the best of many curriculums. I used resources that I thought were more interesting and more conducive to educating them body, soul and spirit. I wanted my children to have the best opportunity to develop their interests and be creative thinkers.

Maybe I should have sent Sarah off to public or Christian school in Grade 9 or 10? That didn't seem like an option for us at that time. The public school where we lived sounded horrible. A parent told me a terrible story of what her daughter had to endure and I didn't want that for my precious Sarah. The Christian school was a half hour drive away and too expensive so I did the best I could. Sarah had enough high school credits so she graduated one year early. I didn't realize she wasn't ready to leave home. She seemed amazingly mature and level headed to me. She should have had a gap year and worked or went to Bible school for a year. I didn't realize she had been too sheltered. Sarah wrote and did well on the SAT (a test of a student's academic skills) and was accepted as a student at Trinity Western University. She attended for two and a half years. Sarah has said she did not feel I properly prepared her for university. The plan was she was to attend TWU for one year and then transfer to any university of her choice. That plan did not happen. Sadly, University was not a good experience for her. Sarah has recently upgraded her high school Math, Physics, Chemistry and Biology so she can pursue other interests. I have apologized to Sarah and she said she forgives me. I am sorry this part of my story isn't happier. I asked God to lead me so maybe in His eyes I made the right choices. I don't know. I guess I will find out in eternity when I see things from His perspective. I am so thankful to God for these precious, beautiful children. I believe God has great plans for their lives and will use them for His glory.

Fox, Shalev, Shane, Savannah, Sarah

Haiti

"Jesus looked at them and said,
'With man this is impossible, but not with God;
all things are possible with God.'"
Mark 10:27

What does a life set free look like? How is life with the Lord Jesus Christ different from a life without Him? What does He give us freedom from? Haiti gave me graphic answers to these questions.

On August 14, 1791 a pig was sacrificed, a voodoo ceremony was performed, and Haiti was dedicated to the devil. At the time of the pact Haiti was known as the 'Pearl of the Caribbean' for its incredible beauty. After selling its soul to Satan it became one of the world's most ugly and impoverished nations in the world. The country is steeped in voodoo. Voodoo is a mixture of African spiritism and witchcraft. On April 8, 2003, President Jean-Bertrand Aristide approved Voodoo as an official religion in Haiti. Voodoo priests can officiate at marriages and other ceremonies. "An ancestral religion, Voodoo is an essential part of national identity," Aristide said when recognizing Voodoo. He said it was a source of national pride. Today Haiti is a nation in complete disarray and disorder. It is unsafe. People live with fear-filled eyes behind razor-barbed wire fences. They live in desperate poverty and are often unemployed, hungry, and hopeless.

In 2008 Kathy Tate, a lady from the church John pastored in Penticton, invited me to help her with a women's conference in Haiti. I had no idea what to expect. We arrived at Port au Prince at night. Someone came to collect us from the airport in a beat up old truck. We climbed in the open back with our luggage. As we slowly drove down the road I had the impression this was the closest I had ever been to Hell. There were no streetlights. People sat amongst piles of garbage along the road. Their faces were lit up by the fires that were lit in old oilcans. The scene was dark and oppressive and ugly. I believe what made it even uglier was the obvious presence of evil.

We were there for ten days. It seemed like an eternity and also such a short time to be able to make a difference. The needs were overwhelming. I hope our visit brought encouragement to some. My heart was grieved over the poverty and broken lives. The fear was palpable. The people seemed to be lost in an apathetic misery. Many stared at us with vacant, fear filled eyes. I am so thankful Jesus gives us freedom from fear.

We drove for about three hours over mountainous, very bumpy roads deep into Haiti. We passed above ground cemeteries where the cement coffins had the ends broken open so people could steal the bones for voodoo ceremonies. As we drove down dusty roads we saw dismal shacks enveloped with razor barbed wire. Ladies from all over Haiti had been invited to the women's conference. Their husbands were mostly pastors and evangelists who were attending a men's conference at the same time. My message to the ladies was about turning away from the worship of anything but God. When I prepared what I felt God put on my heart to say while I was still in Canada I had no idea how relevant that message was. After the message there was an altar call. I was unprepared for the prayer requests. One young woman asked for prayer that she could be set free from demons because her parents had dedicated her to Satan. She told us she was a voodoo queen. She told us she had done unspeakably horrible things. She was tired of the evil spirits forcing her to run naked through her village. She wanted that to stop. Kathy and some other women and I prayed Jesus would set her free. I pray she is still walking in freedom.

We brought suitcases full of clothes to share with the women. When we lay the clothes out for them to choose what they would like we were shocked to see the chaotic "free for all" it became. Seemingly dignified Christian ladies were yanking clothes out of each other's hands. It was a mess. They were in such desperate need.

There is another thing about Haitian culture I do not think I could ever get used to. When a meal was served the men ate first. The women ate next. All the while children with huge, hungry eyes stood watching from doorways and corners. If there was any food left the children would have a chance to eat. I did not want to eat to ensure there would be food left for the children but Kathy said they prepared the food for us and would be insulted if we did not eat, those were difficult meals to eat.

Many people in Haiti are afraid of life and terrified of death. When God sets a person free life becomes an adventure with Him. We have no fear of death because we know it is just an entrance into true life. Jesus destroyed the fear of death and a lifetime of bondage by His death for us (Hebrews 2:14-15). Life forever with God is going to be beyond amazing.

"Eye has not seen, nor ear heard,
nor have entered into the heart of man
the things which God has prepared for those who love Him."
1 Corinthians 2:9

Please pray for Haiti, that Jesus would have mercy on the people and set them free from the traps and snares of the devil. He is their only hope. He alone can give freedom from fear, bondage, superstition, hopelessness, sin and eternal death. True freedom comes from Jesus.

Israel

"This is what the Lord says, He who appoints the sun to shine by day, Who decrees the moon and stars to shine by night, Who stirs up the sea so that it's waves roar - 'Only if these decrees vanish from my sight,' declares the Lord, 'will Israel ever cease being a nation before me.'"
Jeremiah 31:35-36

David Ben Gurion said, "In order to be a realist in Israel one must believe in miracles," Israel's first Prime Minister. He didn't realize the depth of meaning in his words when he made that statement. "Who has ever heard such things? Who has ever seen things like this? Can a country be born in a day or a nation be brought forth in a moment? Yet no sooner is Zion in labor than she gives birth to her children" (Isaiah 66:8). God's promises to Israel are as sure as the sun that rises each day.

Of course the greatest miracle in Israel's history is that the King of the Universe, the LORD of all Creation, the One who prophets spoke about; lived, died, rose again and ascended into Heaven in Israel. Yeshua HaMashiach, Jesus the Messiah, fulfilled every Messianic prophecy about His first entrance into the world. Jerusalem is where the Anti-Christ will one day stand to declare that he is god (2 Thessalonians 2:4). Israel is where Earth's final battle, the Battle of Armageddon, will be fought (Revelation 16:16). Jerusalem is where Jesus promised to return one day to rule and reign over the earth in righteousness (Jeremiah 3:17). That is when He will fulfil all remaining prophesy about the Messiah. No other nation can boast of such an amazing, incredibly supernatural history, present and future.

So why did I go to Israel? God led me of course. In 1986 John had a stopover in Israel for a week when he travelled to India with evangelist Len Lindstrom. John came home saying I HAD to go to Israel. He said I was Jewish. I thought that was ridiculous. To me that was like saying you are Catholic because your grandmother was Catholic. It made no sense. A few years later John suggested I call the Jewish Agency in Vancouver to see if there were any flights going to Israel so we could find a deal on flights. He really wanted me to experience the land. Abraham called back and in a heavy Hebrew accent said, "Rena, I have such a deal for you". He went on to explain about Sar El. He said we would love it. He told us Sar El is a non-profit service organization that brings volunteers from all over the world to help in Israel. We just had to pay for our flights. Everything else, our accommodations, food, tours, even our clothing would be provided. It sounded amazing. He said Sar El would put us wherever we were needed. We could end up on a moshav (farm) picking fruit, helping on a kibbutz, volunteering in a hospital with burn victims or working as a volunteer with the IDF (Israeli Defense Force).

In June 1993 John and I left Sarah (5) and Shalev (3) with Mike and Anne Feenstra's family on their dairy farm in British Columbia for three weeks and flew to Israel. We knew our little girls would be loved and cared for. When we got off the plane in the middle of the night I felt like someone hit me in the face with a wet blanket. The humidity was incredible. Sar El sent a driver to pick us up and drop us off at a Russian Absorption Centre until they could figure out what to do with us. When I woke up I was completely disorientated. It was night when I went to sleep and it was still night. I had slept for twenty-four hours. I couldn't understand why everyone in the room was speaking Russian. Now that I look back on that time, it was amazing to be right in the thick of the Russian "aliyah." "Aliyah" is the word used today for the return of the Jewish people from the diaspora (the nations) to the land of Israel. God was releasing His children from the North just as His prophets had foretold (Jeremiah 13:14-15).

We ended up on what was called a top-secret tank base in Julis near Ashkelon. I'm not sure why it was stressed to us that it was top-secret, as people in Ashkelon seemed to know about it. We were given identification cards (see the photo on the chapter called John) and were told they were our pass to get in and out of the base and to go for meals. We were warned to guard them well because if someone with ill intentions ever got one and had access to the base they would not be coming for lunch.

Being at Julis was an interesting experience. My job was to sort uniforms into various sizes after the wash. I was a bit disgruntled about my job until I felt God whisper to me I could pray over the uniforms. Suddenly my job seemed incredibly meaningful. One morning I went to work and the uniform sorting place was padlocked. No one was around. I went to Allouche, our "madrich" (leader), who trundled me off to the officer's kitchen to help with preparations for a celebration. John had already been barred from the kosher kitchen because he tried to wash the milk dishes and meat dishes in the same sink at the same time. That was the first time we heard yelling in Hebrew. The celebration was going to be a reunion of all the leaders who had once called Julis home. The top commanding officers were going to be there from all over Israel. John hung around with a guy named Marovich who was in charge of setting up for the anniversary at the tank base. He took John to all sorts of cool places all over Israel to collect supplies for the celebration, places that tourists would never be allowed to go. John said, "He treated me like a brother."

Every weekend we were taken on a tour. We hiked up Masada in IDF uniforms. That was cool. At the top we were greeted by a group of excited Japanese tourists who thought we were the IDF. It was pretty hilarious. They insisted on taking pictures of us. We were such a motley crew, ranging in age from an 18-year-old "Dead Head" from Toronto with a mass of long curly hair to a 75-year-old German Holocaust survivor with tattooed numbers on his arm. Masada is an ancient fortress near the Dead Sea where nearly 1,000 Jews lived while under siege from the Roman army around 70 AD. Rather than be captured and enslaved, the Jews chose suicide. It has become a symbol of the Jewish spirit.

The tour of the Yad Vashem Holocaust Memorial in Jerusalem was heartbreaking. It is inconceivable that people could commit such atrocities, but I realize that without Christ the human heart is deceitful and desperately wicked and capable of all manner of evil (Jeremiah 17:9). As our little Sar El group drove through the ancient biblical sites, Allouche sat in the front of the bus telling us amazing stories of Israel's history, like David fighting Goliath. We saw the place where Allouche told us the battle would have taken place. He said nothing has changed. The IDF is still small compared to her giant enemies. It is only God that can protect her. Allouche's commentary was so animated that John and I couldn't help saying "Amen!" after many of his comments! This animated Allouche even further. It was such fun!

Going to the Western Wall was surprisingly emotional. I stood crying with my hand on the wall. At the time, I had no idea why I was crying. Afterwards, someone told me you cannot be Jewish and stand at the Western Wall and not weep. Maybe it was because of the symbolism of the wall? It had endured so much but was still there. Just like the Jewish people. The prayers tucked into the crevices made me think of the hopes and dreams and yearnings of thousands of people who had stood at that wall before me. They cried out to God. They realized that He is the only real Tikvah (hope) for this world.

John and I were dropped off at a bus stop by the Dead Sea to catch a bus to Jerusalem. I still was not convinced about my Jewishness, so when John saw a rabbi walking down a street in Jerusalem he decided this was the perfect time for me to question him. I asked the rabbi, "If my grandmother was Jewish does that make me Jewish?" He asked, "Was she your mother's mother or your father's mother?" I said, "My mother's mother," and he replied, "Then you are Jewish." He said it with such finality and by the look on his face it was obvious the discussion was over. There was nothing left to talk about. What an amazing place to find out I am Jewish. In Jerusalem.

Allouche told us if we went to the Western Wall on Shabbat we would most likely be invited somewhere for Shabbat dinner. A man in a big furry hat and a black trench coat was busily arranging places for people to go. He told us to stand with the Epstein group. I wondered if Epsteins lived in a mansion as the group grew to a large number of people. Epsteins turned out to be a Yeshiva school, a place where students come to study Torah (the first 5 books of the Bible). I guess John looked like a likely candidate. It was great fun. We sat around the table singing and banging on the table to keep time with our music. The Chai (life) in Israel is beautiful.

An "intifada" of sorts happened during my second visit to Israel. "Intifada" is an Arabic word that literally means "shaking off." An intifada is an armed uprising or rebellion of Palestinians against the Israelis and is a term that is used to describe shaking off perceived oppression. An increase of violence started in early September 2015 and lasted until spring 2016. It was known as the "Knife Intifada" because of the number of stabbing attacks. It began when Palestinian activists gathered on the Temple Mount on the eve of Rosh HaShanah to prevent Jews from visiting the site. These activists barricaded themselves inside the Al Aqsa Mosque. Sadly, there were several casualties. My friend Lori Styles from Canada and I were guests at Abraham's Hostel in Jerusalem during that time. One evening we heard screaming and when we looked out our window at the hostel we could see a crowd running and screaming down the street. Shortly after that we heard an ambulance and saw a man on a stretcher being loaded into an ambulance. It was surreal. He was a victim of a knife attack. The streets were deserted at that time, but Lori and I were tired of being cooped up in the hostel so we ventured out one morning into the streets of Jerusalem. The owner of a ladies dress shop was so delighted to see us he practically gave me a dress. I really didn't want a black sundress, but I felt so sad for him I had to buy something. It was lovely imagining how he would be able to go home that day and happily tell his wife he made a sale.

During my second visit to Israel I spent three weeks with Sar El (the same volunteer organization John and I had helped with previously). I was on an army base in Beer Sheva sorting tools with a group of volunteers from all over the world. We were from the USA, Canada, Poland, Germany, Switzerland and Australia. I'm not sure how it was possible but sorting tools for three weeks was actually fun. I joined a Return Ministries Tour and was blessed to see a lot of northern Israel. Return Ministries' goal is to participate in the return and restoration of the Jewish people from the four corners of the earth to the land of Israel. They have just started a program to bless "lone soldiers," young people who come to Israel from the nations to join the IDF. Return Ministries also stands with the Jewish people as advocates for Israel. I didn't know armored buses existed until the Return Ministries Tour. We went to the land they hoped to purchase for a ministry center. I am happy to tell you that since then they have purchased the land and are refurbishing the buildings to use as a place to bless others.

Victoria James led an amazing Bridges for Peace Women's Prayer Tour. One night about ten of us stood on the shore of Galilee and prayed together for Israel and the Nations. I had the impression that we were standing as mighty warriors, daughters of the Most High God. I felt like I was in the company of incredible women of God. So humbling. It was electric. I felt the power of God like never before. Bridges for Peace has various areas of ministry. The volunteers must raise their own support as the staff are not paid. They have a food bank that processes over three tons of food each day. They provide food for about 22,000 people in Israel each month, including immigrants, Holocaust survivors, poor children (both Jewish and Arab), orphanages and Jewish community centers. I was a bit disappointed I only had a chance to volunteer for one day in the Bridges for Peace food warehouse in Jerusalem. But by the end of the day I was thankful

I was only working there for one day, as the volunteers were hauling huge crates of food and preparing boxes for distribution. It was exhausting. The list of all the help that Bridges for Peace provides in Israel is astounding.

Merv and Merla Watson's Jerusalem bed and breakfast was quite unique. People from all over the world congregated there. The Shabbat meals were delicious and our conversations were interesting. One evening I met a lady from Germany who shared with me that the Lord had told her she was to go to Israel because He had an assignment for her on Mt. Carmel and she was planning to go to Mt. Carmel the next day in obedience to His word to her. It sounded like such an interesting trip, so I asked if there was room for me to go with her husband and another lady. She said there was room. I believe it was while we were on our way to Haifa the lady told me the rest of the story. She said God told her three women were going to be reading God's Word and praying on Mt. Carmel. She said God told her He would show her who the third woman was when she was in Israel. It was me. That was a shock!

We stood on a hilltop overlooking the Megido Valley, where the Battle of Armageddon will take place (Revelation 16:12-16). We found scriptures about God's promised restoration of Israel and we claimed them. We prayed Ezekiel 37:9 over Israel -- over the valley of dry bones, that breath would come from the four winds and the dead would live, that God would pour out His Ruach Hakodesh (Holy Spirit) over His people. We prayed that stony hearts would be replaced with hearts of flesh. I don't remember all that we prayed, but it was amazing (shocking actually) that God included me in that time of prayer for Israel.

On my third visit to Israel I stayed with a friend in Jerusalem and then spent a week doing ulpan (Hebrew language school) in the Negev Desert on a kibbutz to attempt to learn Hebrew. If there's language in heaven I hope it's Hebrew. It sounds so beautiful. I bought a book called "The Beauty of the Hebrew Language" by Nathalie Blackman. The author says "chayim" means "life" in Hebrew, but there is also another interpretation, which means "this one life on earth and our second eternal life." Our life to come is affected by every day of this life here on earth. Hebrew has such depth of meanings.

The ICEJ (International Christian Embassy in Jerusalem) Feast of Tabernacles had over 6,500 people from about 90 nations registered. The ICEJ has had "pilgrims" coming from the nations every fall to celebrate in Jerusalem for the past 35 years. The Feast of Tabernacles is a biblical celebration that lasts seven days. It is also called the "Feast of Ingathering" or "Succot" and is a time of rejoicing over the harvest and remembering God's miraculous provision in the wilderness. Booths are built at this time and fruits of the harvest are hung from these temporary shelters. Many families eat their meals in these booths and some sleep there. This festival is a foreshadowing of the Feast that will be celebrated in Jerusalem by all nations during the 1000 year Millennial reign of Christ (Zechariah 14:16). All 6,500 of us had dinner together and praised God in several languages in the desert at En Gedi. It was really a foretaste of heaven, when people from every tribe, tongue, and nation will worship God (Revelation 7:9) together forever.

During my second visit to Israel, the Bridges for Peace women's prayer group visited Kehilat HaCarmel (Carmel Congregation) on the highest point of Mount Carmel near the city of Haifa. Their mandate is "restoring the altar of the Lord on Mount Carmel," based on 1 Kings 18:30. The "kehila" (Hebrew for congregation) is located in the area where Elijah had the showdown with the prophets of Baal. It did not go so well for the prophets of Baal. The congregation was birthed in 1991 in House of Victory, a men's rehabilitation center started by David and Karen Davis who were sent out from David Wilkerson's Times Square Church in NYC. The founding vision for both ministries is based on Isaiah 58:7-8.

> *"...is it not to share your bread with the hungry,*
> *and that you bring to your house the poor who are cast out;*
> *when you see the naked, that you cover him,*
> *and not hide yourself from your own flesh?*
> *Then your light shall break forth like the morning,*
> *your healing shall spring forth speedily,*
> *and your righteousness shall go before you;*
> *the glory of the LORD shall be your rear guard."*

They have a "one new man" vision (Eph. 2:14-16) to share the love of God with Jews and Arabs to help bring reconciliation and healing. Elijah's Cloak is another ministry of Kehilat HaCarmel that helps provide clothing to needy families, as well as the Ravens Basket feeding program that was started to provide food for the needy. Another outworking of their Isaiah 58 vision is the women's shelter for African refugee mothers and children at the Or HaCarmel Ministry Center, next to the congregational sanctuary.

Kehilat HaCarmel also operates the Beit Yedidia Community Center in the center of Haifa where guests from around the world can stay for bed and breakfast. Beit Yedidia primarily functions as a hub of activity for the local body of Messiah. It is in use every day of the week with a multitude of congregational and inter-congregational gatherings held there. I had the wonderful opportunity to volunteer at Beit Yedidia for a month and met some very dedicated, beautiful people who are giving their lives in service for others.

Another significant branch of the ministries of Kehilat HaCarmel is their 12-day intensive Mt Carmel School of Ministry, directed by Peter Tsukahira, Co-Founder of Kehilat HaCarmel, for men and women who are seeking a deeper understanding of the Scriptures and an anointing from God for end-time ministry. The goal of the SOM is to help equip people to take their place in the kingdom as "a people prepared for the Lord" (Luke 1:17).

Kehilat HaCarmel also has an annual 10-day worship and intercession program called Ascend Carmel, as well as ongoing weekly worship and prayer watches. These prayer watches are joined by local Israeli believers, as well as people from all over the world. This is one incredible place!

God provided the opportunity for me to be a guest volunteer with HaYovel in a vineyard for a day on the hills of Samaria. What a blessing to see prophecy come alive. "You shall yet plant vines on the mountains of Samaria" (Jeremiah 31:5). Judea and Samaria are the historical and spiritual heartland of Israel. Biblical history mainly took place in this area. The media calls this area the "West Bank." Many Jewish people live here because they believe the promises of God for the restoration of Israel as foretold by God's Prophets. HaYovel has helped plant vineyards and olive groves to assist Israeli farmers. Many farmers planted, not knowing where they would find laborers to help with the harvest. HaYovel has brought thousands of volunteers over the past nearly twenty years to bless the farmers of Judea and Samaria. We were told that twenty-five tons of grapes were picked the day I helped. Mine was an insignificant contribution as I probably ate almost as many of the incredibly sweet grapes as I put in the basket. The wines that have been produced from these vineyards are now world class and have won many awards.

HaYovel took the volunteers on a mini-tour in the afternoon. We saw Shechem from a hilltop. It is now in the middle of a Palestinian zone called Area A that you cannot enter without IDF guards. There are warning signs that you are risking your life if you go there. This is the area where Abraham, Isaac, and Jacob received the promise that this land would belong to their descendants forever, an Everlasting Covenant that cannot be broken. We could see two very congested and fenced areas in the middle of Shechem. We were told that most terrorists come from this area. This is where pictures are taken of what life is like for the "refugees." The rest of the homes we saw looked very nice. We saw Mt. Gerizim and Mt. Ebal, the place where God gave the children of Israel the promised blessings for following Him and curses for not following Him. Joseph's field and tomb could be seen from the hilltop. As we drove away from Shechem we saw a home (from a distance) being built by a leader in the Palestinian Authority. We were told the estimated cost is in the millions. It was a magnificent, palatial mansion. No further comment.

The Honest Reporting conference in Jerusalem was interesting. It was about fighting bias against Israel in the media. I met incredible people from all over the world. A professor spoke with us about Israel's history from the Balfour Declaration to the birth of Israel. He recently presented an academic paper at The Hague in the Netherlands. He said four other academics pulled out of the conference because his presentation, which supports Israel under International Law, did not conform to their beliefs. The dinner was cancelled as some of the academics did not want to eat with him because of his views.

The tour of the Western Wall Tunnels with a historian was amazing. We had dinner at a unique restaurant in an old Crusader cistern underneath the Old City of Jerusalem. The trip to the Gush Etzion settlement with the former head of the Civilian Department of the IDF was really sad. In the War of Independence in 1948 Gush Etzion was besieged by large enemy forces. Two hundred and forty of the inhabitants of the settlement gave their lives to defend Jerusalem. Gush Etzion was liberated in the Six Day War and its sons returned home.

Kay Wilson shared at the Honest Reporting Conference how she survived a brutal machete terrorist attack that left her Christian friend Kristine dead. She said that act of terrorism robbed her of more than just a friend. She said she lost her sense of humanity when she had no ability to even take care of herself. She was robbed of physical, mental and emotional health, independence, and her ability to provide for herself. Kay wondered how two men who were once someone's little boys could do such things. Where was their humanity? The attackers wanted to kill her simply because she was a Jew. They killed her Christian friend because they assumed she was a Jew. Since the attack Kay said she has an intense awareness of life. She has learned to be thankful, to keep short accounts, to acknowledge the past and the future but live in the present. As she lay on her bed trying to recover from several surgeries, Kay's Jewish friends brought lots of food and said, "May God avenge you." She noticed the Christians did not bring as much food but said, "God bless you. He loves you."

Even though she said she has learned to keep short accounts, Kay said she finds it difficult to forgive. Many Jewish people, especially those who have been seriously victimized in the Holocaust and terror attacks, do not see forgiveness as a righteous response to evil. Today Kay is passionate about bringing international awareness regarding the Palestinian Authority's sponsorship of terror, and she would soon be presenting a report at

Rena Groot

The Hague in the Netherlands. She explained that Palestinian children do not grow up desiring to be doctors and teachers, but instead, their highest aspirations are to be paid killers of Jews. Those who kill Jews are provided free education, medical care, and about $3000 a month.

We visited the Shaarei Zedek Hospital that has been treating patients of every race, religion and nationality since 1902. Dr. David Applebaum was an emergency room doctor who treated dozens of victims of suicide bombings in Israel. He addressed a symposium on terrorism in New York, marking the second anniversary of the 9/11 attack. He concluded his speech with: "From one moment to the next, we never know what will happen in the ER (emergency room), but it's in Jerusalem that real reality occurs." Applebaum returned from the symposium in New York and went for coffee with his 20-year-old daughter, Nava Applebaum, the night before her wedding. A suicide bomber decided to visit the same coffee shop. The murder was a tragic irony. Applebaum had trained both Arab and Jewish physicians and nurses to respond quickly to emergencies. When the attack occurred, the emergency room staff were perplexed as to why Applebaum did not arrive to help. They were devastated to find their beloved mentor and his daughter were both dead.

The people of Israel have remained strong and courageous in the wake of so many tragedies they have had to endure. Israel is now deeply engraved on my heart. It is an amazing, beautiful, historical, vibrant, alive nation. This tiny country, the size of New Jersey, pulsates with life --"chayim" -- and hope --"tikvah." If you have never been to Israel I highly recommend you visit. You will be surprised and blessed. Please pray for the peace of Jerusalem (Psalm 122:6).

China

"Those who know Your Name trust in You, for You,
O Lord, do not abandon those who search for You."
Psalm 9:10

A lice, my 94 year-old auntie-mom, lived alone in her home in Tsawassen, BC. I offered to live with her to help her with her house and her garden. I resigned from
my teaching position at Penticton Christian School at the end of the school year with
the intention of moving in with Alice after the summer. Alice fell that summer and was
taken to hospital. She was given medication that she must have had an allergic reaction
to because her mild dementia suddenly morphed into major dementia. In what seemed

like a moment all plans changed.

Alice had left a living will asking a trust company to take over her affairs if she ever became incapacitated. She had told me she had not left me in charge because she did not want me to be burdened. The trust company brought in caregivers to stay with Alice in her home 24/7. They made meals for her, cleaned her house, and a gardener looked after her massive yard. Everything I wanted to do for Alice was being done by someone else. My moving in with her was no longer necessary. The dementia made visits longer than a few days stressful as Alice could no longer handle too many people around. It was sad.

I had already resigned from my teaching position at Penticton Christian School so I did not know what to do with myself. I had always wanted to go to the Feast of Tabernacles in Israel but had not been able to go because I was teaching every fall. I asked John what he thought of my going to Israel. John was working in Northern Alberta and was rarely home. My children were grown and did not need me. John thought my going to Israel was a wonderful idea. He thought I would love it. I asked him how long he thought I should go and he told me to ask God. I went to Israel for two months. God really does move in mysterious ways. Right after I went through customs on my way back from Israel I noticed people lined up at a counter to have their bags checked for China. I thought that must be so amazing to go to China. God must have been laughing. Within a few months I was on my way to China.

I really had nothing to do, so I applied with Maple Leaf International School in Tianjin, and was hired after the school year began as a high school teacher. Teachers arrived there all year long. Upon my arrival in China, my first thought in the airport washroom is why would someone steal the toilets. There were only holes in the floor. While walking around the city I noticed red lights are a suggestion. Pedestrians do not have the right of way. They are meant to be swerved around. People hang on to the back of motorcycles as they go careening around pedestrians. Such fun for them! China is a cool place. No seat belts, recycling, bicycle helmets, or baby car seats. Such freedom! Taxis charge about $2.00 to take you most places. I mostly walked. Sometimes taxis followed me along the curb waiting for me to get fed up with walking. I had been going to an international church an hour walk from the school. The landscaping was really beautiful so I loved the walks.

I loved high school! I taught Communications to Grades Eleven and Twelve students for a year and a half. One of the assignments the students had was to write a business letter. One young man wrote a very polite letter to other men to invite them to his call girl service. He could not understand why I did not think his letter was suitable. He was the same young man who had a picture with a silhouette of naked ladies dancing on a poster to advertise a graduation party. Maybe I should not have been surprised when the principal told me one of my students was being put through school by his father's brothel business. Perhaps that was common in China? The young man with the interesting business letter and poster was my prime suspect as the son of this brothel business owner. You can imagine my surprise when I met his parents at a career fair. They were a very sweet, humble, quiet couple of schoolteachers.

One Sunday one of Jackie Chan's pilots from America shared at the international church I attended. Jackie Chan is a famous actor, martial artist, film director, stunt man and producer. He has appeared in over 150 films, many of which have been shown in Western nations. The message from Danny was simple, but powerful. It was about how our choices determine our destiny. Danny said his father chose to start hanging around with prostitutes instead of his mother and ended up in prison. He did not elaborate on exactly why he was in prison. One day the prisoners were served delicious bread. The dad got back in line for a second piece. A guard grabbed him by the arm, hauled him out of line, yelled at him and told him he knew he was only allowed to go through the food line once. The dad obviously had some Christian background because, as he sadly told his son during a visit, he was reminded of the Bible verse, "For a whorish woman a man is reduced to a piece of bread" (Proverbs 6:26). Danny said his dad had been a strong, healthy man. He was now a broken, sick, frail man. I asked Danny if he would like to share his message with my Grade 12 students if I had permission for him to come to the school. Danny agreed. Guess which student I especially hoped the message would speak to?

The principal was excited about Jackie Chan's pilot coming to our school. He wanted the other Grade 12 classes that were available to listen as well. Danny asked me if he could read from the Bible. I asked another teacher who replied, " Sure. Why not?" The principal was away the day Danny came to share, but the principal's Chinese secretary came to listen. She was fine with the photos on the screen and the talk, until Danny pulled out the Bible to read how a king's disobedient choices lost him his kingdom and eventually his life. Immediately after the presentations I was sent a text message to report to the vice principal's office as soon as possible. The vice principal kindly reminded me that this is Communist China. The police would be called to the school if any of the students complained. I told him I took responsibility for the Bible story as Danny asked permission and I gave it. The police never did come. I am so thankful for the opportunity those students had to hear that message. I hope it makes a difference for someone.

Rena Groot

One of my colleagues at Maple Leaf International School was a beautiful First Nations lady named Elizabeth Calder. She was expecting a baby and unfortunately her husband was in Africa so she was pretty much alone. I felt God lead me to ask if I could help her in any way. She was so thankful I offered. I ended up going to Tianjin City with her every Saturday for over a month for her checkups at the hospital. That involved one hour bus, train and taxi rides each way. It was exhausting for Elizabeth. Once there was a false alarm and we thought the baby was arriving so another lady and I went to the hospital with Elizabeth. We shared a tiny couch for a night at the hospital. The last time Elizabeth and I went for her checkup it was discovered that the umbilical chord was wrapped around the baby's neck and we would have to stay at the hospital for Elizabeth's emergency caesarean. I am quite squeamish but when Elizabeth asked if I would like to cut baby Lovey's umbilical chord I thought it was such an honor to be asked I made myself do it. I was so relieved I did not pass out. The principal told me to stay with her and had other teachers cover my classes. I soon found out if you don't have someone bring you food at a hospital in China you don't eat. My new assignment was to find food for the new mommy. I had to walk along a busy highway to a little shopping mall to find food. It was a harrowing experience, walking along the road with cars racing past, however, I was glad to be there for Elizabeth.

Allan Cousell was a man who encouraged, impacted and inspired others. Allan's wife is a professor at Tianjin Medical University. They attended a church I sometimes visited in Tianjin City. Allan's funeral in Tianjin City on April 9, 2017 was a beautiful testimony of a life lived for God. We were told Allan was in a terrible car accident 17 years ago. He nearly died. God showed him a vision of people on their way to Heaven. God turned him around and showed him the people behind him and informed him he could go to Heaven at that time or stay for the ones he saw behind him. He chose to stay.

We were told Allan lived with courage, had the guts to say what needed to be said, and had wisdom and deep trust in God. Allan became "daddy" to many lonely students from many nations. He showed students what a man of God looks like. He laughed and cried with them. He pulled them from dangerous, even suicidal, situations. He told the students he believed in them. Many made it to their graduation because of his wise counsel and encouragement not to give up. When others saw a foreigner Allan saw a friend. Many are now in the Kingdom of God because of his life.

Some of these students read "Dear Daddy" letters they wrote to honor him at his funeral. These letters were sent from Ethiopia, Sri Lanka, Kenya, and many other points of the compass. We saw an inspiring video sent from a young man in Africa. Allan's life blessed and touched many lives. We were told he loved God and people, that he was kind, loving, positive, a mentor, a strong warrior, and that he left a beautiful legacy. Because of his love for God and others his testimony is being heard around the world.

Some of the students for whom Allan was "Daddy" were from Sri Lanka. These students had gone back there to practice medicine. Allan went there to visit them and while there in Sri Lanka he contracted dengue fever and died because of complications that led to a heart attack. He will be greatly missed. The funeral was a beautiful tribute to a great man. When I hugged Christine, Allan's wife, she said she feels like God is carrying her. Christine told us Allan's message to the living would be, "Love God, love others. Live your life with no regrets."

"And God will wipe away every tear from their eyes;
there shall be no more death, nor sorrow, nor crying.
There shall be no more pain, for the former things have passed away."
Revelation 21:4

The international church I attended had people from over one dozen nations in attendance. Sadly, if you held a Chinese passport you were not allowed to attend. I went to a Three Self Patriotic Movement Protestant Church for a special Christmas program. The building was packed with people who sang the hymns with passion. Someone sitting beside me interpreted for me. That particular church had a pastor who did not seem afraid to speak truth. The three things the government gave the recognized church permission to achieve was self-governance, self-support (independence from financial aid from foreigners), and self-propagation (independence from foreign missionary work). The government was in control of the Three Self Patriotic Movement. They place their people into pastoral positions so are able to infiltrate and control much of organized Christianity. People who belong to this church are required to give their primary allegiance to the government. There are other people who meet in homes and cafes and caves to hear the Word of God. This is the unregistered or underground church. I have heard it is the fastest growing church in the world. The photo for this chapter is a young lady who is a member of the underground church in a northern province of China.

Please pray our Chinese brethren will remain strong and faithfully follow God all the days of their lives. There are more stories about China, but to protect people you will have to wait until Heaven to hear them. Actually, even better, you will get to meet these precious people. You will love them!

Thailand

"I do not pray for these alone,
but also for those who will believe in Me
through their word"
John 17:20

While teaching in China I had a one-week holiday coming up. I wondered what I would do that week. I had a fleeting thought that I should go to Thailand. I dismissed the thought as I told myself I had no idea where I would go in Thailand or what I would do. My Chinese friend Jane invited me to travel with her in China for the holiday. I thought that would be wonderful as Jane could speak Chinese and knew lots of interesting places to travel. Jane had such a funny habit of talking to Chinese people in

English and then turning and speaking to me in Chinese. We had so many laughs together. I miss my Jane. About a month before the trip Jane informed me her parents wanted to travel with her that week so she could not travel with me. In China, parents trump everything. For example, my friend Connie told me her mother wanted her to be a doctor. Connie did not want to be a doctor, but her mother said she was going to stop eating until Connie enrolled in medical school. Dr. Connie is not excited about being a doctor, but she decided it was a better option than watching her mother starve.

I lived in a very small apartment on the international school campus, so the thought of sitting there for a week by myself was very uninspiring. The thought of going to Thailand flitted through my mind again. I had the same conversation with myself. I had no idea where I would go or what I would do. Surprisingly, I got an email from Watchman for the Nations even though I was not on their email list. They do not know how they got my email either. It was an invitation to a Watchman for the Nations Global Gathering in Chiang Mai, Thailand, exactly on the dates I had off school. That was amazing. Of course you know I went because this chapter is called Thailand. The first night we were told there were over 1,200 people from thirty-nine nations present. For some reason I had the feeling there should be forty nations. I have no idea why I thought that. The next day they announced that Nepal had just arrived and there were now forty nations. I felt God's peace knowing we were all present.

Many of the people were from restricted access nations so we were asked not to take pictures. If their pictures showed up on social media it could endanger their lives. Many tribal people wore their traditional clothing and got up on the platform to greet us. Some sang, some danced, some prayed. It was incredible. One man from China stood on the platform and told us he was wanted by the authorities. He had been running and hiding for years and God told him to stop running and hiding. He told us about miracles where God protected him. Friends had called him and asked him to never contact them again. Their lives would have been endangered. He said some brothers then stepped into his life and told him they would stand with him no matter what. They were willing to stand with him even to the point of going to jail or to death. Then, the most amazing thing happened. A group of men stepped up on the platform and stood around our Chinese brother. They were the men who had pledged their lives to stand with him. I cried.

There was a young Chinese man who danced with all his might before the Lord. His tiny wife sat cross-legged on the floor holding their small child. She looked adoringly at him. They looked so poor. I could not imagine the hardships many of these people must have endured to get to Thailand. It was a joy to see these precious people have this time of blessing and encouragement.

There were so many different languages spoken but we all spoke the universal language of love. There were huge tables full of resources in several languages in the hallway. We could take whatever we wanted. A Thai friend, Alicekoi, and I took piles of Thai tracts and walked through a mall that was connected to our hotel and handed them out. We went into a Persian carpet store and shared with two Muslim men about Jesus. They said if we brought them Arabic materials about our God they would read them. We went back to the stash of materials and found a Bible and other materials in Arabic to take to these men. I hope we see will them in Heaven.

A few of us visited a young lady who works with YWAM and is helping rescue very young girls from prostitution. She could not tell us much about her work except to say she was in the process of rescuing three children. Thailand is a center for child sex tourism and child prostitution. Domestic and international authorities have worked hard to protect children, but the problem has simply exploded and is a serious issue in many Southeast Asian countries. This ugliness and depravity makes me long for the purity of Heaven. Don't people perpetuating this abuse realize these are children?! How do they look in the faces of their own children? I pray many will be convicted of the depravity of child prostitution and even speak against it.

The photo of the beautiful Thai couple was taken in a Hmong mountain village about an hour north of Chiang Mai. About ten of us travelled in the back of a squishy taxi to get there. The couple are wearing traditional wedding clothes. I love their story. The young man left his village with his parents when he was three years old to live with his family among other Hmong refugees in Minnesota. He started a Facebook friendship with a girl from his village in Thailand. The friendship blossomed and he came back to Thailand to marry her. The young woman was going to America with her new husband. She spoke no English. I love their story.

Mexico

*"Pure religion and undefiled before God and the Father is this,
to visit widows and orphans in their distress"*
James 1:27

The North and South Belize YWAM teams were stranded in the middle of Mexico. It was the summer of 1984. We sat on the side of the road waiting for the steering wheel and the brakes on our bus to be fixed. A man on our team pulled out his guitar and started playing. Soon a crowd gathered. The crowd was mostly women and children. The next thing we knew the women divided us into groups and took us to their homes for tortillas. If you saw their homes you would realize what an incredible act of kindness and love this was. I am sure the women prepared all the food they had to feed us. It was incredibly humbling to accept their generosity. We had such a celebration! The joy and love was palpable. This act of love by these beautiful Mexican people gave us a glimpse into their heart and culture.

In 2012 Savannah & I went with a bus-load of mostly teens from Penticton to help build houses in Vicente Guerrero, 200 miles below the Tijuana border in Baja Mexico. If you need help on your building project Savannah and I are pros. The photo is of Savannah in Vicente Guerrero, Mexico. The children loved her. Most of our Live Different team were teens. Live Different was originally a Canadian charity established in 2000, but by 2005 it began its international operations. Live Different is primarily a youth empowerment program. We had fundraisers to make money to buy building materials and supplies for the people we helped who lived in abject poverty. Many were farm workers who stood for hours baking in the hot sun only to bring home about $4 USD a day. It was an enormous blessing to be able to see my Mexican family go from living in a big tent with a dirt floor in a field to living in a beautiful little home with furniture, bedding, kitchen supplies, and food. It was so exciting to see people given keys to their homes.

God surprised me in the Fall of 2017 with a trip with DMI to Mexico City. Disciple Making International (DMI) is a Mennonite Brethren ministry that has seen thousands of people pray to receive Christ. Half our team was from Canada and the other half was from a Bible School in Paraguay. Our entire focus was evangelism. I loved it. We went into communities to tell people about the love of Jesus. Our team shared our stories (testimonies) alongside national believers who interpreted for us. We visited people in their homes and presented the plan of salvation. Many responded to the life-giving message of the gospel.

At one point my interpreters and I, two beautiful Mexican teens, were standing by a rickety gate telling an elderly couple how much God loves them and how Jesus gave His life so they could live. Suddenly it seemed like the ground was heaving and rippling under my feet. It was the weirdest sensation. I was sure I was imagining things. The elderly man looked astonished and told the interpreters he saw the telephone pole behind me swaying. It was a powerful 7.1 earthquake that toppled buildings and killed over two hundred people. Thankfully we were in a rural area and not close to the epicentre. It is interesting what goes through people's minds when death could be imminent. My first thought after I realized we were experiencing an earthquake was we need to hurry up and give these beautiful people the opportunity to meet Christ. Their meeting Him in eternity could be imminent. They did pray with us to receive Christ as their Savior.

We worked closely with the evangelical churches in the areas. They had teams of people who were prepared with follow up lessons for anyone who made a decision for Jesus. The interpreters were part of the follow up teams. They had already met the people we evangelized and prayed with them in Spanish so there was a level of trust that had started to develop between them.

The churches sometimes fed us lunch at a church building and sometimes took their Canadian and Paraguayan "evangelists" to their homes. It reminded me of the kindness I first saw in the people of Mexico years before when we were in YWAM. People who were very poor sacrificed their chickens to prepare what looked like a feast to bless us. Again, I was humbled by the beauty and love and graciousness I saw in my Mexican brothers and sisters. Dr. Wyman, who graciously read the manuscript for this book, said people often see Mexico as only poor and needy. When she was in Guadalajara in 2016, she was impressed with the beauty she saw. Dr. Wyman said she and her husband went to the most spectacular shopping centre they had ever seen. Please pray for Mexico, that God would protect His people, draw many to Him, and His Name would be honored throughout the land.

Africa

*"Whatever you did for one of the least of these
brothers and sisters of Mine You did for Me."*
Matthew 25:40

Our lives are made up of stories. Some are heartbreaking. Some are joyous. Some are surprising. What I am about to tell you was a very unexpected story that encompasses all of the above. While flying home from Mexico, out of curiosity, I asked God if there was someplace He wanted me to go to next. I did not really expect an answer, so I was surprised when I heard God whisper Africa. It was not a whisper I heard with my ears, but more like a voice I felt resonate inside me. Africa??? Why would I go there?

What would I do? I trusted that if this was really God speaking to me He would show me His plan.

When we met Ingrid told me about her many missions adventures. I must have looked very interested because she recommended I talk to International Messengers (IM) about the possibility of my going on a missions trip with them. I looked at their website. IM is an "evangelical, interdenominational missions organization comprised of an international staff team committed to making disciples of all nations through partnering with local churches to renew, train and mobilize believers for active involvement in reaching the world for Christ." I read that they were going to have a youth camp in Kampala, Uganda, for a week in January 2018. I felt God wanted me to go. I applied and was accepted.

While waiting for the American team to arrive and meet me at the Entebbe airport in Uganda I thought about the daring rescue that took place there in 1976. The Popular Front for the Liberation of Palestine hijacked an Air France plane with 248 passengers. The Ugandan government under Idi Amin welcomed and supported the hijackers. The hijackers demanded the release of 40 militants imprisoned in Israel and a few other assorted terrorists from other countries. They released all non-Israeli passengers, but threatened the Jewish passengers and the Air France crew with death if their demands were not met. Because of this threat, "Operation Entebbe" code-named "Operation Thunderbolt," was planned. The Israeli Defense Forces (IDF), under the direction of the Israeli intelligence agency Mossad, flew transport planes 4,000 km through the night and rescued 102 of the 106 hostages. It was a miracle. Yonatan Netanyahu was killed during the rescue operation. He was the older brother of the current Prime Minister of Israel, Benjamin Netanyahu. The rescue is sometimes called "Operation Yonatan" in his memory. It was surreal standing in that airport realizing that is where that event had taken place.

There were five North American leaders for the International Messengers youth camp. We each had a group of ten young people from Sojourn Church to love and mentor for a week. We stayed at the African Children's Choir compound and had a blast together. I seriously don't think I have ever laughed so much in all my life. It was wonderful seeing God touch the lives of these beautiful young people. The American team went back to the United States after the week and the Canadian team (me) stayed on for two months with International Messengers. God had some very interesting plans for me.

Before I went to Uganda I saw a Facebook post about the Happy Totos Children's Home and School near Kampala. I contacted the director, Cossy Kiyingi, and was invited to visit. The Happy Totos is an incredible place. There are over fifty orphans who have been rescued and hundreds from the surrounding Muslim village who have been given the opportunity to have an education. A 3 year-old girl was discovered tied in a bag in the jungle. Her father, a witch doctor, had just killed his wife and kept his daughter there for days to be used as a human sacrifice. When she was found the police did not know what to do with her. They contacted Cossy and he welcomed her into the orphanage. She has been given a loving family, a home, a hope and a future. God has since led me to start a Go Fund Me for the orphanage. So far He has provided over $17,000. The Happy Totos have been able to dig a well, buy food and clothing, medicine, mosquito nets and bunk beds, pay school fees for the older students (the school only goes to grade six), buy land and plant crops. So amazing! Here is the link if you would like to help. https://www.gofundme.com/change-a-life-make-a-difference.

Shakira was in my youth group at camp. One Sunday we planned to meet after church to talk about her dream of becoming a teacher. I wanted to help her but when I went to the bank machine before church I found out I did not have enough funds to buy a cup of coffee. I sadly told Shakira I could not help her. That evening Paul, the manager of the guest house where I was staying, invited me to go with a group to visit Miracle Center, the church he attended. That was an experience. There were probably a few thousand people congregated under huge lights on a gigantic field. Visitors from other countries were invited to come up on the platform and greet the church people. I told them I was from Canada and that I heard they prayed for Israel. I thanked them for their prayers and told them God promised to bless those who bless Israel. That greeting was televised all over Africa and around the world by satellite. The pastor then asked all the people to pray for a need each one had. Thousands of people paced the field crying out to God for various needs. I prayed God would provide money for Shakira to go to school. After the prayer time I was surprised to hear the pastor call me up on the platform again. There was an envelope sitting on the podium and he said God wanted me to have it. He then asked me to pray for Uganda. The next morning I called Shakira to ask if we could meet for coffee. It was so exciting to hand her the envelope that said, "To Shakira. Love from Jesus" with one million Ugandan schillings in it. There was more than enough to money to pay for school and with the extra money she bought food for the Happy Totos Orphanage.

There was a Friday evening Bible Club for the children of Wabigalo, Kampala. The photo at the beginning of this chapter is of me helping round up neighbourhood children for the Bible Club. They were so excited to be there. One evening the children were dancing and singing with all their might while waiting for the Bible lesson to begin. Finally, after waiting for a lengthy time, I asked when the lesson was going to start. I was informed I was leading it. Surprise! Thankfully God warned us to be instant in season and out of season. The children were more than happy to be actors in a very impromptu Bible story.

Pastor Kostya from Sojourn Church suggested I join a team for an outreach to street kids. It was heartbreaking. Children lay all over the street in filthy clothes on dirty sheets. Some walked around in a daze from sniffing airplane fuel. The team went into a small building where the children sat to listen to a message and have lunch. I was asked to share with them. Afterwards a young girl gave me a note that said, "Thank you for coming -- us street kids will never forget you." She was the only girl in the room. Shadia later told me she hid under piles of clothes in the market at night so she would not be seen. I contacted Cossy to see if Shadia could come to the orphanage. Of course he said "yes." I invited Shakira to come with me to pick up Shadia from the street. I thought Shadia would be more comfortable having someone with her who could speak Lugandan. Shadia carried all her possessions in one small backpack. She was so grateful to be rescued. Shakira ended up staying at the orphanage with me for the week and interpreted when I shared with the children in Chapel. Shakira is a natural teacher. She taught me how to steam food with banana leaves and wash clothes in a pan. There was no running water so we had to collect water. Shakira, Harriet (Cossy's wife) and I stayed in one room together. We were like three sisters. It was such a blessing to be with the Happy Totos.

The Loving Hearts baby orphanage was beautiful because of the precious babies, but sad because they had been abandoned and there was little hope for a family for them. Some of the babies had AIDS. They desperately wanted love and attention. If you put a baby down to rescue another crying baby, the one who was put down would immediately cry. There were five of us visiting the baby orphanage. We mostly just sat on the floor with our arms and laps full of babies.

I visited a place for juvenile delinquents called The Children's Prison. This was a home for teens who had been apprehended by the law for various crimes. I went with a group that visited once a week. A doctor volunteered each week and provided medical care to the teens. Volunteer teachers gave the students English lessons. One of The Children's Prison ministry team told me about a teen-aged Muslim girl who had been apprehended and was in prison. She was a third wife. The two other wives accused the teen of murdering one of their children. One of the workers said the other wives were probably jealous and made up the story to get rid of the young wife. The prison was run by the government. We were told they sometimes did not send food for weeks at a time. If it was not for the Christian volunteers bringing food every week there were times the children would have had nothing to eat. There are a few more stories about Africa but I will tell you about them when we meet in heaven. They are stories of God's amazing love and kindness in the lives of His children.

Greece

"And this is love: that we walk in obedience to His commands.
As you have heard from the beginning,
His command is that you walk in love."
2 John 1:6

Did you know the original language of the New Testament was Greek? Does that seem strange? You would think it would be either Hebrew or Aramaic, the languages Jesus and His disciples would have spoken. Greek was the "trade language" during the years the New Testament was written, from about 50 to 100 AD. Most of the books of the New Testament were written in the nation of Greece. Corinth, Galatia, Ephesus, Philippi, Colossus, Thessaloniki are cities in Greece. John wrote the Book of Revelation while imprisoned on the island of Patmos in Greece.

Teaching English to refugees and visiting the homeless in Greece was not at all on my radar screen. My daughter Savannah was going to Israel with Birthright and wanted to visit Greece. I offered to accompany her. I thought that would be safer for her. While Savannah was in Israel I thought it would be cool to help with Muslim refugees. I applied with Kitab World Education and was accepted. Kitab is an international non-profit organization dedicated to working with refugee teens and young adults residing in Greece. Kitab students are provided with the resources and mentorship for continuing education, certifications and skills for job readiness. With an individualized education plan, Kitab students are matched with college students in Athens and with professionals from anywhere around the world and work towards certification in the careers of their choice." While there on my own I had the opportunity to teach students from Turkey, Syria, Iran, and Afghanistan in the "Hope Café," The students were so interesting. Each had an incredible story.

Haman attended my English classes. He had been a schoolteacher in Turkey. He said one day 140,000 people were fired from their jobs. He was one of them. There was no notice or explanation. He suspects it was because the 140,000 were known as non-supporters of the leadership of Turkey. Haman said he knew he had to flee the country as he realized the next thing awaiting him was arrest and imprisonment. He had to leave his wife and baby behind in the care of his family. He hopes to one day be able to send for them.

Tamim (name changed for his protection) was another one of my students. He drove me to the airport on my last day in Greece and as we drove he told me his incredible story. He was wanted by the Mafia and the Taliban in his home country of Afghanistan. He had been a policeman and had refused to accept bribes and look the other way when crimes were being committed. The Mafia, armed with AK-47 assault rifles, had a shoot out with the police. A man was killed. Tamim's brother was blamed, arrested, and sentenced to twenty years in prison for the crime of doing his job as a policeman.

Tamim met a lovely Muslim girl at a meeting. They exchanged emails and soon became friends. One day Tamim was shocked to get a frantic message from his friend. She was only 17 years old but was about to be forced to marry a 55 year-old man. She said if Tamim didn't come to her rescue she would be dead. Tamim drove 1000 km through dangerous terrain to rescue the woman who is now his wife. Her family was not impressed. They sent people after them to kill them as they said the young woman had brought dishonor to the family by running off without permission. They escaped, but sadly, three years later, their three-year old son was kidnapped and killed. It was meant as a warning. Tamim, his wife and baby daughter fled for their lives. They could not fly out of the country as their names had been reported to the authorities. They had to go overland and hope for the best. Thankfully, by God's grace, they arrived in Greece. Tamim said he had an interview with the government to decide if he would be allowed to stay in the country or not. He said after he shared his story the men who were interviewing him all got up from their chairs, hugged him and welcomed his family to Greece. He said the papers that could have taken months to be processed took weeks.

I brought a pile of gospel tracts to Greece and as I walked down the streets in Athens I left the tracts in conspicuous places. One day I could not find the coffee shop where the students were waiting for their English lesson. I must have walked for about half an hour farther than I should have when I realized I must have walked past the meeting place. My excuse was the windows on the shop were dark and there were no distinguishing signs. I retraced my steps and found the coffee shop. There was a billboard on the wall outside the coffee shop and I had left a tract there. So, my students must have watched me leave the tract and then watched me walk away. They must have wondered about me. The next day all the tracts along the street were gone. I pray someone's life was touched.

Artur Cillpaka started an outreach to refugees and homeless people in Athens called "Refugees Refuge." I had the opportunity to walk with him a few times. Artur said the mild climate makes it easier for people to live on the streets. Artur said he lived on the streets for a month just to experience what these people have to deal with on a daily basis. He showed us the park bench he slept on. We handed out sandwiches and drinks and tried to find the right size of clothing to give to people. One couple on the street lived in a giant cardboard box in an abandoned entranceway to a store. They had somehow lost their home and the box was all they had left. I am so thankful that one day, when Jesus is ruling and reigning in righteousness, there will be no more homelessness.

When Savannah and I stayed on the island of Santorini we went to a hilarious play about a Greek wedding. The audience was part of the play. We were greeted with hugs and kisses and exclamations of, "Cousin! So glad you could come!!! How nice you came all the way from Canada!!!" We were invited to join the wedding celebrations by feasting, dancing and smashing plates. So much fun! The scenery in Greece is so beautiful. We went on a day cruise on a schooner that moored by mineral springs that bubbled up from the bottom of the sea. I took the photo for this chapter off the coast of Santorini in the Aegean Sea from our schooner. Passengers were invited to jump overboard and swim in water as warm as a bathtub. It was funny being in water that the Apostle Paul was once shipwrecked in. We hiked on a blackened island that was formed by a volcano. We were comforted to hear it had not erupted in years.

I was only in Greece for a few weeks. It is crazy what you can squash into a short amount of time. Please pray that God will pour out His Spirit on the people of Greece and draw them close to His heart.

The Highway of Holiness

"Beautiful for situation, the joy of the whole earth,
is Mount Zion, on the sides of the north,
the city of the great King"
Psalm 48:2

This painting is my idea of what it might look like on the Highway of Holiness. "And a great road will go through that once deserted land. It will be named the Highway of Holiness. Evil-minded people will never travel on it. It will be only for those who walk in God's ways; fools will never walk there" (Isaiah 35:8). There are mountaintops, cavernous valleys, and deep waters if we stray off the road. It is the way God calls His children to walk. The Highway of Holiness can be a lonely road, but it is beautiful. It will lead us home.

Rena Groot

When you choose this road you will find where the real journey begins. Sometimes our journey can be colorful and exciting. Sometimes it is meandering and may be surprisingly mundane and even boring. That is life. There are mountaintops and valleys. There are places that travel with you in your heart long after you have left them behind. As God leads His children on the Highway of Holiness we may find ourselves in some unexpected situations.

There are roads we would NOT choose, but God in His wisdom chooses them for us. It's crazy how our lives can change in a heartbeat. It was 1978. I was teaching Grade Two at Sir Alexander Mackenzie in St. Albert. John invited me to a Chuck Girard concert at the Kinsmen Fieldhouse in Edmonton. Chuck Girard is known as a pioneer in Contemporary Christian music. He founded a band called Love Song, the first Christian band in the U.S. I absolutely loved his music. While the crowd stood worshipping God I thought this must be as close as you can get to heaven on earth. As we left the fieldhouse I was so euphoric I felt like I was flying. As we walked to the car I noticed a row of posts that separated the parking lot from the grassy area. On an impulse I decided to jump up on a post. It was about a foot and a half high with a sharp angled top. I leaped from the post I was on to the next post. I am not sure how I came up with such an insane idea. Of course I slipped. I fell on top of the post on my right side. It was a miracle I didn't die on the spot. I found out later that my right lung had collapsed and my right kidney was so badly lacerated the bottom third was severed. I lay on the ground bleeding internally. John was mad at me because he thought I was pretending to be hurt. He didn't find the joke amusing. He walked off and left me. I think he was in shock and denial. Thankfully some people came by who asked if I needed an ambulance. I said yes. When John heard the ambulance he realized I wasn't joking and jumped in the ambulance to go to the hospital with me.

The Bible says that out of the abundance of the heart the mouth speaks. I was delirious, but I know I kept thanking Jesus that by His stripes I was healed. The next ten days were a blur. I was on morphine for pain and I was hooked up to many machines. My auntie-mom did not think I was going to live. Someone visited me in the hospital and brought a book called *A Shepherd Looks at Psalm 23*. I read and prayed through the entire book. Jesus had never been so real or so close (no it wasn't the morphine). I felt like I was His broken lamb and I was in need of His healing touch. When a lamb is injured the shepherd carries him. I definitely felt like I was being carried.

A doctor wanted to operate and remove my kidney. He said it was so badly damaged it would not heal properly. This is such an amazing part of this story. One day while watching the get-well cards from my students dancing on the wall (morphine does weird things to me) I felt God's touch on my right side. The burning heat was so intense I asked God if He could please turn the heat down a bit. I asked politely. I didn't want Him to turn it off completely because I knew He was healing me. While I was still in the hospital I was sent for further x-rays which showed my kidney completely whole, with a fine white scar-line to show where God performed the surgery. It was a miracle!!! Having walked in the valley of the shadow of death I can promise you God will be with you. We don't need to be afraid. He will never leave us or forsake us.

Another road God led me down was leading tour groups. When it is not incredibly stressful, it is a lot of fun. I have been leading tours in Western Canada through the Canadian Rockies all the way to Vancouver Island for parts of a few summers for different tour companies. Leading tours is a great way to meet people from all over the world. I must say I feel inadequate for the job. That is actually a blessing because that makes me depend on God. On one particular tour I asked the guests to think of their most favorite place to visit and why it was their favorite. I told them I would come around and write down their response and share all the beautiful destinations with the other guests. All forty people pretty much had different places they loved for very different reasons, all the way from a beach in Bali to a castle in Scotland. The next day, just before we said goodbye at the cruise ship terminal (my guests were going off on an Alaskan cruise), I asked, "What if there is a place that is even more beautiful than all the places mentioned yesterday? Would you be interested in going there?" They were interested. "What if it didn't cost you anything? It was all expenses paid?" Now they were really interested. I then said something like, "This place is incredibly beautiful. Here is some information about how to get there." Then I gave each one a tract. That was the only tour I did that on. I hope God led me to do that. Honestly sometimes it is difficult to discern if something is God or just my own zany idea. I hope it was for someone who will be standing in Heaven because I was (again) willing to look foolish.

Being a tour manager means being away from home, traveling with people you don't know and sometimes being in a culture you are not familiar with. Even when it is an English speaking country some of the words have very different meanings. Next summer I have been asked to lead a tour in Newfoundland. I am so excited. Did you know, "Who knit you?" in Newfoundland means, "Who are your parents and where do you come from?" "Twacking" is when you are shopping, but you really don't want to buy anything. You just need a couple of hours to gaze at items for sale. Shop owners love it when people come twacking because they might find something they want to buy. "Chummy" is a word used to replace the name of something. For example, if someone is working on a car and they need a 15 mm wrench they might say, "Pass me the chummy." Then hopefully the person they are speaking to is a mind reader. I would think twice about having surgery in Newfoundland.

When I was in Belize people kept asking "You alright?" I thought I must look really sick or awful because so many people were asking if I was alright. Someone laughingly explained that "You alright?" means "How are you doing?" The acceptable response is "Up till now."

I was only home from Israel for a few days in 2018 when I flew to a Gate 1 Convention in San Antonio, Texas. Gate 1 is an international tour company Dani Pipano started in Israel. He established the Gate 1 Foundation to help with the educational needs of children in developing countries. Gate 1 has tours in Asia and Pacific, the Middle East, Latin America and North America. While sitting at an airport in Vancouver waiting for my flight to Toronto (it was unfortunate this was the best flight the company could find for me) to connect to San Antonio, Terry asked what I do. I told him I am a teacher, tour manager, writer (well, I am writing this book), and I work for the Department of Eternal Affairs. We had a great conversation and I am so thankful to tell you that one day you will have the joy of meeting Terry in heaven. He was planning to go home armed with the little tract I gave him to tell his wife Ann about Jesus. So what seemed to me to be flights out of my way to get to San Antonio were exactly where I was supposed to be to meet Terry.

A pastor's wife in Israel prayed over me the morning I left Haifa. She told me she believes what God is still going to do in my life will be even greater than what He has done in the past. I had never spoken to her before. How could that be possible? That seems incredible. I can't imagine. God has already done so much. Maybe she means in eternity? I know God's plans for us are amazing. I don't know where God will lead me. You don't know where God will lead you. I know I have entered through the narrow gate and am already quite a way down the Highway of Holiness. I want to encourage you with the words from Matthew 7:13-14, "Enter through the narrow gate. For wide is the gate and broad is the road that leads to destruction, and many enter through it. But small is the gate and narrow the road that leads to life, and only a few find it." Be one of the few. God's plans for you reach into eternity. They are far more amazing than you could ever imagine. Trust Him. He loves you.

The Storms of Life

"Do not fear, for I am with you;
do not be dismayed for I am your God.
I will strengthen you and help you;
I will uphold you with My righteous right hand," says the Lord.
Isaiah 41:10

As you know, life rarely goes smoothly or according to plan. Thankfully it usually isn't as scary as this picture of a supercell tornado cloud over Taber, Alberta in May 2018. Sometimes troubles buffet us with gale force winds. How do we rise above the storms of life? How do we escape the sometimes overwhelming feelings of discouragement and depression? Do you sometimes feel too unimportant, marred, or insignificant to be useful for the kingdom of God?

I understand. I have been there. What can you do when you are bombarded by the lies of the enemy? You know the lies. You are not good enough, smart enough, pretty enough, handsome enough, athletic enough, witty enough, etc. I am sure you can think of a lot more. These lies are designed to incapacitate you. They are meant to keep you from fulfilling your God-given destiny. You do not have to buy the enemies lies. You may be being fed the lie that your happiness lies elsewhere. News flash! If the grass looks greener elsewhere maybe it is because it's astroturf. I hope these few important keys to freedom I have discovered will encourage you to rise above where you are now.

First, resign the position of "Administrative Director of the Universe." You are not required to be in charge. You must trust God to lead you and let Him have control of your life. In order to find freedom, "Submit to God, resist the devil, and he will flee from you" (James 4:7-8). Satan comes to rob, steal, kill and destroy. His goal is to separate you from God and ultimately destroy you. You must do exactly what Jesus did when confronted by the devil. He spoke the living, powerful, sharper than a two-edged sword, Word of God. John 8:32 states "You shall know the truth, and the truth shall set you free." God's truth says you are beloved. Jesus gave His life so you could live. You are unconditionally accepted. If you have repented of your sin and asked Jesus to be your Savior you are adopted into His family forever!!! The King of all kings and the Lord of all lords loves you with an everlasting love. Such amazing grace.

Secondly, when the enemy tells you something God has called you to do is impossible, you can boldly claim, "I can do all things through Christ who strengthens me" (Philippians 4:13). When you are afraid you can quote, "God has not given me a spirit of fear, but of power, love and a sound mind" (2 Timothy 1:7). Do not allow the enemy to rob you of the joy of the Lord. It is your strength. If you do not have joy then by faith praise and thank Him that His joy is your strength (Nehemiah 8:10). We walk by faith and not by sight. I was not feeling especially strong or joyful while volunteering at a guesthouse in Haifa. There was a lonely tiger in the zoo behind the guesthouse who cried every night. I felt so sad for him. His forlorn cries often kept me awake so I felt exhausted before the day began. I wanted to rescue him. I thanked the Lord that His joy was my strength and claimed that I could do all things through Christ who strengthens me. Surprisingly, people at the guesthouse commented that I exuded joy. What a miracle. That was not from me. I take no credit for it. It was totally from God. If you look to your own abilities and strength you will be defeated. You need God. You cannot walk the highway of Holiness unless you abide in Him and walk in His strength. Without Him you can do nothing (John 15:5). You could not even take your next breath unless He gave it to you.

Thirdly, "Faith comes by hearing, and hearing by the Word of God" (Romans 10:17). I believe this is what Jesus meant when He told us to abide in Him. You must abide in His Word. "In the beginning was the Word, and the Word was with God, and the Word was God" (John 1:1). You will be "transformed by the renewing of your mind" (Romans 12:2) as you meditate on His Word and abide in Him. You will become like Him. False beliefs will dissolve. The lies of the enemy will be exposed and fall away. Jesus offers healing for your heart, soul, mind, body and spirit. He is the only one who can make this offer. He alone can transform you and change you into someone who brings glory to God. Holiness is a process. If you fall down get up. Ask for God's forgiveness, wisdom, help, guidance and keep walking. He alone has the words of freedom and eternal life. When you are tempted to fear and doubt God's love and care for you the words, "He is my refuge and my fortress…in Him will I trust" (Psalm 91:2) are powerful. When I was alone in China I had times when the spirit of fear would try to overwhelm me. It was amazing how as I claimed, "When I am afraid I will trust in you" (Psalm 56:3) I could feel the fear dissipate. God advises us to meditate on His Word day and night. He knows it will bring us health and wholeness. He says we "will be like a tree planted by the rivers of water, that brings forth its fruit in season…" (Psalm 1:3).

Finally, rejoice always. Determine that you are going to praise God for everything. "In everything give thanks for this is the will of God" (1 Thessalonians 5:16-18). I think that is impossible without God's enabling. Trust God. I mean REALLY trust Him. Recognize that you are a part of God's story. Honestly, if He can use me He can use anyone. I am so thankful that God has set me free. I have been set free from the lies of the enemy. That does not mean that he does not attack. He does. Especially when I am not feeling well or am tired. The enemy loves to kick us when we are down. He is a cruel bully. When you are in a vulnerable place be especially vigilant. "Put on the whole armor of God to stand against the wiles of the devil" (Ephesians 6:10-20).

God has done far beyond anything I could have asked or imagined in my life. He has translated me from death to life. He has rescued me from the kingdom of darkness and brought me into the kingdom of His dear Son (Colossians 1:13). If you are a child of God you no longer belong to the darkness. You have been rescued. God's plans for you are beyond amazing. He has you where He wants you. Unless you are in a life-threatening situation be content where you are. God has you in your own personal custom-designed "Boot Camp." You are being fashioned into someone who will one day rule the nations with the King of kings and Lord of lords (Revelation 20:6). His purposes for you are far beyond anything you could ever imagine.

Rena Groot

So, dear reader, when the storms of life come crashing around you, and they will, praise God because you are being transformed into the image of Christ. How amazing is that? God loves you. He promises to never leave you or forsake you. He is with you always, even to the ends of the earth. You can trust Him. He will not give you anything beyond what you can endure (1 Corinthians 10:13). Do not trust in your own strength. Only God can keep you safe in the storms. He is the only One with the authority to speak to the storms and say, "Peace, be still."

I hope my story of a life set free helps you have a bigger picture of God's incredible mercy and kindness. I pray you will be encouraged to love and trust Him more. I hope you have gained a deeper sense of the love of God and your incredible value to Him. I look forward to meeting you in Heaven and hearing your stories about God's amazing grace in your life. I pray you will dwell in the secret place of the Most High, under the shadow of the Almighty (Psalm 91:1) and that you will forgive as you have been forgiven (Ephesians 4:32). May the love of God fill your heart so you will exude His love to others (1 Peter 4:8) and may you have compassion for those who are walking in darkness. May your light shine so brightly others will see Jesus.

Your life has an eternal purpose. You cannot see it all now but I know by God's Word it is amazing. "Eyes have not seen, nor ears heard, nor has entered into the heart of man, the things which God has prepared for those who love Him" (1 Corinthians 2:9). You are an infinitely precious treasure to God. I pray God will encourage you and bring beauty where there may have been ashes in your life. I pray yours will be a life set free (Romans 8:21) so all of God's highest and holiest and most beautiful plans for your life will be fulfilled. The final chapter of our lives has not been written yet. The puzzle pieces are still being placed. I am trusting God that the final chapters of our lives will be amazingly beautiful for His glory. One day the trials, the hardships, and the evil of this present life will be over. One day the kingdom will come and the King will rule and reign in righteousness. One day we will see Him in His beauty and majesty.

One day
Soon
there will be no more tears
no more pain
no more evil
no more babies being slaughtered
no more children being abused

no more racial conflicts

no more religious persecution

no more poverty

no more selling of people's bodies and souls

no more human depravity and man's evil hearts.

We will be like Him

and it will be more beautiful and amazing than we could ever imagine.

So

the most important thing

in the Universe

is knowing Jesus as your Lord and Savior.

Everything else

is irrelevant in comparison.

Call on Him.

You will be saved.

Your story can be of a life set free!

Trust Him.

He loves you.

I hope to see you in Heaven, beloved.

Love,

Rena

Made in the USA
San Bernardino, CA
08 May 2019